FOR TEENS & YOUNG ADULTS:
MANAGING STRESS, PRESSURE AND THE UPS AND DOWNS OF LIFE
Information, Encouragement and Inspiration

Jennifer Leigh Youngs, A.A. · Bettie Burres Youngs, Ph.D., Ed.D.

from the SMART TEENS-SMART CHOICES series

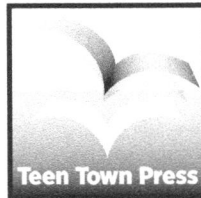

Teen Town Press
www.TeenTownPress.com

an imprint of Bettie Youngs Book Publishers, Inc.

BYB
BETTIE YOUNGS BOOKS

Cover Graphic Design: Adrian Pitariu and Beau Kimbrel
Text Design: Beau Kimbrel
Teen Consultant: Kendahl Brooke Youngs

TEEN TOWN PRESS / www.TeenTownPress.com / Teen Town Press is an Imprint of Bettie Youngs Book Publishing Co., Inc.: www.BettieYoungsBooks.com; info@BettieYoungsBooks.com.

If you are unable to order this book from your local bookseller or online, you may order directly from the publisher: info@BettieYoungsBooks.com.

PRINT ISBN: 978-1-940784-80-9
DIGITAL ISBN: 978-1-940784-81-6

10 9 8 7 6 5 4 3 2 1

Library of Congress Cataloging-in-Publication Data Available upon Request.
Youngs, Bettie Burres. Youngs, Jennifer Leigh.
Summary: Information, inspiration and self-help skills to help young adults managing stress, pressure and the ups and downs of daily life.
1. YA literature. 2. Stress Management. 3. Peer Pressure. 4. Life Skills for Daily Living.

Also by the Authors for Teens and Young Adults

FOR TEENS & YOUNG ADULTS: How Your Brain Decides If You Will Become Addicted—Or Not

FOR TEENS & YOUNG ADULTS: The 10 Commandments and the Secret Each One Guards—FOR YOU

FOR TEENS & YOUNG ADULTS: Setting and Achieving Goals that Matter TO ME

FOR TEENS & YOUNG ADULTS: The Power of Being Kind, Courteous and Thoughtful

FOR TEENS & YOUNG ADULTS: How to Be Courageous

FOR TEENS & YOUNG ADULTS: How to Have a Great Attitude

FOR TEENS & YOUNG ADULTS: Growing Your Confidence and Self-Esteem

FOR TEENS & YOUNG ADULTS: Caring for Your Body's Health and Wellness

FOR TEENS & YOUNG ADULTS: Having Healthy and Beautiful Hair, Skin and Nails

FOR TEENS & YOUNG ADULTS: 365 Days of Inspiration

FOR TEENS & YOUNG ADULTS: Inspirational Stories and Encouragement on Friends and the Face in the Mirror

FOR TEENS & YOUNG ADULTS: Inspirational Short Stories and Encouragement on Life, Love and Issues

FOR TEENS & YOUNG ADULTS: My Journal on Life, Love and Making a Difference

FOR TEENS & YOUNG ADULTS: 12 Months of Faith: A Devotional Journal for Teens

FOR TEENS & YOUNG ADULTS: A Teen's Guide to Christian Living: Practical Answers to Tough Questions About God and Faith

CONTENTS

Introduction   ix

1. **Teens Discuss What Causes Stress in Their Lives**   1
   The Party . . . Turned Out Different Than I'd
      Planned by Tandi Stevens, 16
   Is Your Life Stressful?
   Common Stress Triggers: Ages 12 to 20

2. **What Is "Stress"?**   9
   Stuck in the Crossfire by LaToya Jones, 17
   STRESS 101: The 3 Phases of Stress
   "Fight or Flight": The "Alarm Phase" of Stress
   "The Coast is Clear!" The "Resistance/Adaptation Phase"
      of Stress
   "Burnout": The "Exhaustion Phase" of Stress

3. **The Three "Side Effects" of Stress**   17
   The Trouble with a Goddess by Gerard Hamilton, 17
   How to Recognize the Physical, Emotional and Behavioral
      Signs and Symptoms of Stress
   Virtual Practice: How Does Stress Affect You?

4. **How Do You [Re]Act When You're Stressed-Out?**   23
   You Snooze, You Lose! by Rob Lawson, 15
   What to Do When Stress Takes Over
   Virtual Practice: Stopping the Cycle of Stress

5. **Do You "Thrive" on Stress?**   27
   Globe-Trotting, Jungle-Braving, Tundra-Probing
      Boyd Matson! by Joshua Thomas, 15
   Virtual Practice: Are You a Stress-Seeker?

6. **Stress: Cool or Ghoul—is Up to YOU!**   31
   Not Two of a Kind by Leah Matheson and Karen Billings
   Virtual Practice: Your Reaction to Stress is Up to YOU

7. Coping Skills: The A + B = C Test for Clear Thinking   35
     A Date with Destiny by Jon Branson, 16
     Stress Affects Your Destiny, Too!
     Thinking Clearly—and Logically—Can Help
       You Stay Calm and Cool Under Pressure
     Virtual Practice: Using the A + B = C Process

8. Coping Skills: How to Be a Positive Thinker   41
     The Night the Power Went Out by Jamie Dykes, 14
     Seeing the Bright Side of Things Can Help You
       Redirect Stress
     Virtual Practice: How to Change a Negative Thought
       to a Positive One

9. Coping Skills: Quick and Easy Steps to Solve Problems   47
     Sonja and Sabrina—and Kyle Thurman! by
       Sabrina Va Arnem, 16
     A 5-Step Approach to Solving Problems Effectively
     Virtual Practice: How to Be a Problem-Solving Sleuth

10. Coping Skills: "Self-Talk"—How to Talk to Yourself
When Stress Sets In   53
     Juliet—and Her Romeo by Brianna Reed, 17
     How to "Talk Out Loud"
     Virtual Practice: Talking Your Way Through a
       Stressful Situation

11. Reaching Out to Others: Who Are the Members of Your
Stress-Management Team?   57
     Family: Members of the "A" Team
     Anything but Normal by Craig Buell, 16
     Four Important Ways Family Members Lessen
       Your Stress and Make a Big Difference in Your Life
     Virtual Practice: Naming Your "Home Team"

12. Friends: On the Team—and the Pep Squad, Too!   67
     Having a Couple of Friends is Better than Just One
       by Barbara Allen, 14
     4 Ways Friends Help You Through Stressful Times
     Virtual Practice: Who Among Your Friends
       Helps You Through Stress?

13. Prevention and Intervention Skills: Great Ways to
    Take Care of Yourself   71
        The Importance of Nutrition and Sleep
        Food Is the Body's Fuel: Three Ways "High Octane"
            Combats Stress
        5 Stress-Busting Benefits of Exercise
        SLEEP: Stress and Your Zzzzz's
        Virtual Practice: Food, Bod and Zzzzz's

14. Prevention and Intervention Skills: Cool Ways to
    Chill Out (and Relax)   81
        3 Cool Reasons to Melt Stress via Relaxation
        Mental Imagery: Reducing "Brain Strain"
        Virtual Practice: How to Train Your Mind to Take a
            Mini-Vacation

INTRODUCTION

In this book, young people (ages twelve to twenty) talk openly about the stress and pressures they face in today's times, as well as ways to best manage stress, and as importantly, use it to their advantage.

Of course, no one has to convince you that life is stressful! From coping with the pressures of getting good grades at school, to passing the test for making (and keeping) friends; from finding a part-time job, to having a life once you do; from deciding where you and your friends would like to hang out this weekend, to deciding where you'd like to go to college (or for job training); from finding time to do all the things you have to get done, to having leisure and "down" time for yourself; from meeting the needs and expectations of parents, teachers and activity coaches, to setting and achieving goals of your own, life can be extreme-edge hectic! So much so that teen Geoff Granger labeled it a "balancing act," while Tandy Mann phrased it the "juggle of struggles" and Cindy Morris called it "Zoo-ville in Teenville."

Whatever name you give to keeping up with your life as a young person—regardless of the ups and downs that stress creates—you know you'd better be cool: You've got to cope. Consider this book your guide for doing just that.

Have you ever had a day when you felt overwhelmed, down-and-out, or simply "at wits end" or "too out of juice" to effectively cope with the situation at hand? Were you suffering a disappointment, feeling betrayed or nursing a broken heart? Was there a time when you had a million-and-one urgent things to do—and not enough time (or desire) to accomplish them? Or, things didn't turn out as you planned—or you had no plans—and everyone else, it seemed, did? Has life thrown you a curve ball, and you don't know what to do about it, nor whom to turn to? On those days when stress sets in, when anxiety lingers, when the pressures mount, when your cool has turned to ghoul, the skills in this book will help you:

- understand what stress is (and isn't);
- examine how you respond to stressful times (and determine how effective that is);
- determine how your stress shows itself as physical, emotional and behavioral symptoms;
- check out some terrific (and time-tested) intervention and prevention strategies to minimize stress and stay cool under pressure; and,
- learn ways you can use stress to your advantage.

Learning how to cope effectively with stressful situations is more than a good feeling. Handling stressful times in positive ways gives you the confidence to confront other stressful encounters. The more you build a storehouse of positive experiences of seeing yourself as successfully handling difficult times in positive ways, the better able you are to handle other tough times.

Having said that, it's important to remind you that, while many young people can handle the day-to-day stress of life, some stresses and pressures are too much for anyone to handle alone. Should you be facing times that are simply overwhelming, rather than suffer alone or resort to doing things that are self-destructive, we urge you to seek help. This is especially true in cases of physical, emotional or sexual abuse, suicidal feelings, eating disorders, depression, pregnancy and/or using drugs or alcohol.

If you're uncertain where to go for counseling, turn to an adult (whether a parent, teacher, school guidance counselor or clergy person) whom you feel you can trust to direct you to the proper place. Also, many schools provide peer crisis counseling, and there are any number of toll-free hotlines that offer young people valuable information and can direct you to other sources of help, as well.

CHAPTER 1
Teens Discuss What Causes Stress in Their Lives

Being a young person in today's times is not without its ups and downs, which create, in the words of teens, "the land of overwhelm." Virtually all young people—of every age and background—have worries and concerns that contribute to the stress and pressures they feel in coping with the many things going on in their lives. From acing the test to figuring out what sort of work or career you'd like to go into; from getting along with your parents to trying to decipher if that second glance from that special someone means he or she likes you (or was simply glancing in your direction), stress is "a way of life," as sixteen-year-old Tandi Stevens found out after the party she planned with the hopes of getting to know a certain guy, didn't exactly turn out as planned.

The Party... Turned Out Different Than I'd Planned

I sit alone in the aftermath
in a 1 A.M. world.
Empty soda cans, used paper plates,
candy wrappers, stains on the carpet.
Everyone's gone.
This isn't what I had planned.

Just a little casual party for friends
deliberately put together
for a chance to be in your presence.
Hoped you'd think I was cool, pretty,
worth getting to know
and want me to be your girl.

I could tell you enjoyed the party.
You came early,
stayed late,
talked with everyone,
laughed, danced and sang songs.
Then left with that other girl.

I sit and stare—at nothing in particular
too sad to laugh, too hurt to cry,
peeling off the sparkles I'd so carefully placed to adorn my skin.
I'd secretly hoped you'd find me cool, pretty,
worth getting to know.
Guess you didn't.

This room for my party,
once filled with laughter and all my huge hopes,
is now just an empty space
amplifying the ache of my lonely, broken heart.
You didn't find me cool, pretty and worth getting to know.
And it's another—and not me—that you want to be your girl.

Tandi Stevens, 16

Is Your Life Stressful?

Have you ever found yourself in a similar predicament—one in which your expectations didn't turn out as you'd hoped? Such times are sure to make you feel disappointed, sad, even confused as to what went wrong.

What's going on in your life that makes it stressful? Take a moment now to reflect about what's stressful in your life.

We asked teens nationwide to talk to us about what, in particular, they think makes life stressful. Here's their take on the "top" causes of stress in "Teenville."

Carrie Linn, 16, Winter Park, Florida: "Most stressful is the balancing act: Being a teen means that you're always trying to meet the expectations of others—parents, teachers, activity coaches and friends—while wanting to do things your own way. You need to assert your own "voice;" I mean, teens have wants, needs and desires, too. And sometimes what others expect of you—from the things you're supposed to be accomplishing to the way you're acting or behaving—are in conflict. It's always a push and pull, a tug of war: You may want to make your own decisions, but you know that someone—and not you—is really in charge. All they have to do is dangle the power of a grade or the car keys over your head—and you know it's so."

Wanda Groff, 17, Chattanooga, Tennessee: "It's always being self-conscious—having acne, wearing braces, a constantly changing body, emotions bouncing around at will—and all are played out in the 'spotlight' so to speak. Everybody's watching. It's a time when being self-confident and giving off an air of self-assurance is necessary, but tough (and you're judging yourself, and hard on yourself, too). This sense of double-identity makes you feel out of sync with yourself, like you're not true to yourself. It's easy to feel bad about yourself because you know you're supposed to 'be yourself' and take your own lead—but you also know the consequences of not being one of the crowd. You can feel like a fake, a fraud, like you and your life is a big lie. Worse, you want to scream out about these things, but instead, sit on them, harboring them until you're sure no one can possibly know how you're feeling and by then, you're too mad at everyone for not reading your mind and knowing how upsetting this duplicity is to live with.

Greg Willis, 15, Toledo, Ohio: "I think the need to have friends dominates all the issues. A huge amount of time and energy is spent on trying to fit in and have others like you. Without friends, you have no life. So figuring out how to get along with all the different personalities, and then learning the 'rules' for getting along is a really big stress."

RaNelle Nelson, 16, White Plains, New York: "Hoping for love: You look around you and see a teen couple, and it just looks so cool to think that someone could be walking you to your class, saving a seat for you at lunch, always knowing you already have a special date for special events going on. You have someone to kiss you and someone to just be there. So when you don't have someone special, you feel that a big piece of life is missing. A special someone is a constant search."

Rianna Sharrit, 15, La Jolla, California: "The love thing— having love or not having love—is the most stressful. If you don't have someone special, you feel left out. But you quickly find out that finding someone to love isn't stress-free either. And, you come to understand that practically everything about love produces stress—whether finding it, keeping it, or breaking up or making up. And, you discover that you've got to make a lot of compromises and a lot of concessions if the relationship is to be fun. And, you hope that it is not going to be just chaotic—one that brings just constant upheaval. You look around and see that some of your friends are always sad or upset because they aren't happy about what's going on in the relationship. A lot of the ups and downs are too draining. Love can be a very stressful thing— both when it's great and when things aren't going so great."

Tyanna Peyton, 15, St. Joseph, Missouri: "Time demands are what makes things so stressful. Having too much to do and not enough time (or stamina) to do it is always an issue for teens. Everyone kind of forgets that having this mega-schedule is sort of a setup for doom-and-gloom from the beginning, because the truth is, you'd like to spend this supposedly 'best time of your life' sleeping. A teenager's body would like to sleep 'til noon. It's not like you wake up every day full of energy and just raring to go get things done."

Brad Bentley, 18, Alexandria, Maryland: "Personal power: Being a teen means you want to be in charge of your life, but more often than not, you feel like a puppet on a string. While on some days you feel like you are, on most days you feel as though you have no control over what happens, so it can be easy to just let others take control. But it ticks you off when they do, especially if they make choices for you and don't consult you first. As a teen, having any great amount of personal power is an illusion."

Betsy Little, 13, Sheboygan, Wisconsin: "Definitely, worrying about friends. Being a teen means that often you're concerned for your friends, especially for the things they're dealing with, like parents in the midst of a divorce, and especially those with big personal problems of their own, like doing drugs or drinking problems. For friends with problems of their own, you worry about them, but for the most part, you don't exactly know what to do or where to turn to get help for them—especially when most of the time you've been sworn to secrecy and so you find that you've promised a friend you won't reveal her problem—which can be as serious as bulimia, pregnancy, drug or alcohol abuse, or emotional or even physical abuse. It's very stressful to be a loyal friend, to want to help but feel powerless to help."

Scott Perry, 17, Syracuse, New York: "Money problems: Being a teen means you're always short on money. If you have a part-time job, you don't have as much time to be with your friends, and you have even less time for yourself given that there's always so much homework and things to do. Most parents pay for the basics and then some, but there are so many things you need money for—such as a special outfit for a date or something special, to go a school trip or special event like a dance or prom or go with a ski club, or even having those things that help you fit in with others. Most all of my friends—guys and girls—wish they had more money."

Janetta McGhee, 15, Salt Lake City, Utah: "A teen's life is filled with constant anxiety: keeping up grades, completing classroom and homework assignments, being able to answer questions in class; thinking you may not be as smart as you'd like to be; being uncertain about what college to go to and whether or not you'll be accepted there.

There's also the worry that maybe college isn't going to be right for you and you'll just end up wasting time and money, and that maybe you should enter the job market once you're out of high school instead. Even then, you wonder what special skills, if any, you possess, but you're never quite sure how to find out for sure. It's a time of serious confusion."

Conrad White, 16, Rapid City, South Dakota: "Career and job concerns always make it to the top of the list for most teens. There is a great deal of turmoil over not knowing what to do with your life. You always hear, 'The sky's the limit,' meaning you can do anything, but knowing there are so many options doesn't make your decisions easier; in fact, it makes them much, much tougher. Sure you'd like to be president of the world, but what if it's your destiny to be Thoreau, or a surf bum. How do you know, and who's to judge?"

Marissa Hewitt, 17, San Bernardino, California: "One's family is always a big stress for teens. Making time to have fun and be close with each family member never seems to happen—but you know it's supposed to. Also, it's a huge emotional drain to be in an argument with your parents, as is being caught in the middle of parents who are separated or divorcing. Problems at home spill over to everything else you're doing—and to the way you're feeling. It's tough to separate yourself from the stress and strains going on in your family. Family stress becomes your stress, too. But it doesn't replace your own stress; it just adds to it."

Kevin Pauls, 18, Safford, Arizona: "Sorting out values. You're forever dealing with what you hear and know to be important and worthy values, but then you see them ignored and violated. And this happens not only in hypothetical situations like the movies or on television, but even by those in leadership positions who are charged with setting a good example for others. It's like there's right, wrong, more right and more wrong. While you'd like there to be a consensus on what's right and wrong, you learn that it depends upon the situation. So when someone asks you what you believe in, you find you're not quite sure. But, you'd like to be very sure."

Virtual Practice: What Overwhelms You?

After reading how teens characterize the stress of teen life, did you find yourself thinking, "That's the way I feel," or "That's not one of my stressors, but it is for my friend," or "That hasn't happened to me—yet"?

The following list shows what young people at each age find to be the things that trigger stress for them. If you are fifteen, you may want to skip ahead to the stresses listed by fifteen-year-olds and see how they compare to those you are feeling. Then, you might want to look at the "last year" and see how you've fared with the stresses you've "left behind." And you might also want to peek one year ahead—just to see what's coming up! After all, it's never too late to get a heads-up on being cool!

Common Stress Triggers: Ages 12 to 20

Age 12:
- Fear of being selected first (and having to lead) and fear of being picked last (seen as being disliked or unpopular)
- Fear of failing in school and not passing into middle school/junior high
- Fear that other kids won't find me likeable and worthy of their friendship
- Fear that others will criticize or make fun of me
- Fear that I won't have many friends
- Fear of losing a best friend

Age 13:
- Fear that a friend will tell my "secrets" to someone else
- Fear of not being able to keep up with others my age, such as not batting as well as everyone else on my baseball (or softball) team, or not doing as well as the others in my class
- Not understanding the changes my growing body is undergoing (and wondering if they are "normal")
- Concern that my "moodiness" means that I am not as happy as I'd like to be—or as I'm "supposed to be"
- Fear of not doing well—most especially if others are watching, such as being called on in class, or performing in athletic competitions (like school sports)

Age 14:
- Not understanding my changing body and wondering if I should believe what my friends say is the way things are "supposed to be"
- Fear that teasing by friends means that I am "disliked," unpopular
- Fear of the sexual feelings I am experiencing
- Concern about whether I am as happy as I am supposed to be

Age 15:
- Fear of others judging my body or my sexuality (such as in "tomboy" or "too sissy")
- Fear of exposing my changing and growing body (such as when shopping with friends, or showering in P.E. class)
- Fear of being challenged to a fight, or even getting in a verbal confrontation

Age 16:
- Fear of being disliked or unpopular
- Fear that another boy or girl will try to take my "sweetheart" away from me, or share a secret of who I consider someone I'd like as a boy/girlfriend
- Fear that I won't ever get my driver's license, get to drive a car, pass a grade, get into college, find a job or a boy/ girlfriend
- Fear that my family is not a "happy family"

Age 17:
- Worry about not liking school or finding it important
- Concern about my ability to get along well with others— boyfriends, girlfriends, classmates, teachers, parents, family members (or, that I compromise too much in order to be liked)
- Fear that I'm not in a "best family" (believing that other families are happier or are "more together" than my family)

Age 18:
- Fear of "not being okay"
- Fear of being made to feel insignificant by others (such as by teachers, or employers or employees at a part-time job)
- Fear of not ever being able to earn enough money for the things I want and need
- Fear that others will control me as I begin to live my own life
- Fear of not passing all my classes to graduate with the rest of my classmates
- Fear of not knowing what to do when I get out of school
- Fear that my parents won't "let go" so I can go out in the real world on my own

Age 19:
- Fear that my parents won't be there for help, support or advice
- Fear of being on my own "for real"
- Fear that I didn't take school seriously enough and learn all that I should have
- Fear that I don't have the skills or knowledge I think I need to make it in "the real world"

- Fear that I won't make it in college
- Fear that I don't have any friends left (because they've all gone off to college or work or moved away)

Age 20:
- Fear I won't have enough money
- Fear I have a boy/girl friend
- Fear I won't get a good job
- Fear I don't make a good impression on others

After reading through the stresses consider how they compare to your own. What other "stresses" would you add to the list, for example:
- to be in an argument with a close friend—or my parents;
- when I've loaned money to a friend who refuses to repay it;
- when a friend tells a secret or betrays me in some way;
- when a rumor is circulated among my friends about me.

Cool is Up To You!

Knowing that others are feeling some of the same things that you are can relieve some of the "fears" associated with wondering if you are "normal." This is good to know because while there many things you can do to lessen stress, you can't make all stress go away. However, you can learn how to manage yourself in relation to it. Throughout this book you'll find a good number of skills and techniques to help you do just that.

The next chapter will help you understand more about what stress is, and isn't.

CHAPTER 2
What is "Stress"?

Stress. We hear the word and use it a great deal, but what is it really? If someone asked you to define stress, what would you say? Maybe you associate it with events like taking a final exam; the adrenaline rush of being the focus of attention at an important competition in a sports activity; being on center-stage during a school play; or, you've got the closing arguments in your school's debate club city championship. Maybe it's that sense of anxiety you have when you need to "face up," "square off," "confront" or "level" with someone, such as with a teacher or your parents because you've broken a promise or not followed through on a certain commitment. Maybe it's that sinking feeling of having an argument with a best friend or the nervousness of not being quite dressed and ready for your date—who is knocking on your door!

While situations such as these can certainly cause an "I'm stressed" response, they are just that: a situation, an event, a happening. While you can't always control or change the event (it's your turn to get up and give that oral report in front of the class), how you respond is under your control. For instance, in the case of the oral report, you can be as prepared as you can possibly be; you can start your day by having a good night's rest, eating a good breakfast, and as an extra confidence boost, looking especially cool that day. Stress, on the other hand, is its own agenda: It is the body's physical, mental and chemical reaction to the circumstances you're facing. No matter what kind of stress-creating factor it is that you're facing—your first kiss, or facing a near head-on collision with a fellow classmate as you make a mad dash to get to class—the same reactions go off in your body. This is good: Your body readies itself to deal with the situation at hand. If, for example, you step off a curb and suddenly an unexpected car wheels around a corner and nearly hits you, it's highly likely that within the flash of a instant, your body will command you to leap out of the way.

And, of course, stress can overwhelm you to the point of not being effective. If, for example, you study for an important test, but on the day of the test you draw a blank, not remembering even the most easy and common facts! So, it's important to learn all you can about coping with stress in positive ways and not let it get the best of you.

If someone asked you to define stress, what would you say? Some teens define it as confusion, turmoil, even excitement. Perhaps LaToya experienced all three of these her "first love," dropped her for her best friend.

Stuck in the Crossfire

Kevin Larson, a guy I liked for nearly three whole months before he even noticed I was alive (even though I'd made it very obvious to him the whole time!) finally asked me out! He was my very first love.

I thought everything was just great between us. We were boyfriend and girlfriend for four months when suddenly he just dropped me for my very best friend, Karina Wells. My best friend! I'd seen that happen to others, but it never crosses your mind that it will happen to you.

When we broke up, I cried and cried. I was sad, mad, confused, miserable without him and indignant, too. But Kevin acted like he didn't care at all about my feelings. He paid no attention to me, just went on about his business, happy as a clam about his new girlfriend, my (and now "ex") friend.

Then, just two weeks later, just out of the blue, Kevin Larson broke up with his newest sweetie Karina Wells. This I found out when he handed me a letter as we passed each other in the hall one day. I was surprised to get a letter, and though I did my best to act like I could have cared less about receiving it from him, I made a straight beeline into the girls' restroom as fast as I could so I could read the words written by the love of my life—even if I was mad at him.

It was a great letter! Kevin told me that he loved me and only me and that he no longer wanted to be with Karina. I was thrilled of course, but still curious. I mean, did he really miss me so much and that was the reason he broke up with Karina—or did she dump him? To tell you the truth, while I was relieved to have him say he wanted me back, I was a little confused, too! I mean, while I was happy that he broke up with Karina, there was the thing about his having dumped me in the first place. And, there was the matter of Kevin wanting us to get back together. Should I just go back, be sweet and tell him how much I missed him, or should I make him work really hard to get me back? All the other kids at school knew the full story, so I couldn't just go back without a fight and lose my self-respect. Should I tell him, "No way! Get lost. You had your chance!"? These are all really important things to consider. And besides, one of his good friends, Rick Torres, had been making eyes at me like he's interested in me, and Rick is pretty cool. Going out with Rick would be a great way to get back at Kevin. But then, my heart belongs to Kevin...

As you can see, it's a tough decision I have to make, one that is being battled out between my heart and my head. I'm stuck in the crossfire, and boy is it stressful:

My heart: "You see! I told you Kevin loves you!"
My head: "Be careful. You know he left you for another girl."
My heart: "Oh, don't worry about that now. What's important is that he wants you back. And besides, you know how good it feels to have him ask you to come back to him."
My head: "Go slow. Your turmoil is sure proof it may not be right."
My heart: "But he wants YOU, YOU, YOU! Be happy, don't worry!"
My head: "A week ago he wanted Karina Wells."
My heart: "But now he wants you!"
My head: "Kevin double-timed you."
My heart: "Yes, but he can be so romantic and sweet."
My head: "He may do it again. Why risk getting hurt again?"
My heart: "Oh, I'm sure he'll never do it again. He said he loves me."
My head: "He's proven himself as someone you can't trust."
My heart: "But I miss him. I want him back."
My head: "Take your time; think it over."
My heart: "If you don't act fast, Teresa Amos will snatch him up! You saw her flirting with him."
My head: "He is a big flirt. I'm suggesting you don't go back."
My heart: "But I love him."
My head: "You're doing just fine without him."
My happy heart: "Love is a wonderful thing. It makes me happy."

What a see-saw! It's been thirty-eight hours and fifty-five minutes since Kevin Larson asked me to get back together with him. And I'm still very stressed out, not knowing what to do!

LaToya Jones, 17

STRESS 101: The 3 Phases of Stress

Most people think stress is having to confront a particular unpleasant or tough situation. Technically, these anxiety-filled events—such as taking a big test, taking your driver's license test, asking out a certain someone or having an argument with a good friend—are called "stressors." The "wear and tear" they cause us is the "stress." Regardless of whether the stressor is a biochemical insult (such as using drugs or alcohol); a physical injury (such as getting in a fight or falling and breaking your wrist); or confronting something you fear or someone who makes you upset, the body responds the same: It is thrown into a "stress reaction."

This reaction has three distinct phases, each one named after that which it does, basically, in response to the incoming stressor. These are:

1. The Alarm Phase,
2. The Resistance Phase, and
3. The Exhaustion Phase.

Stress can be a good thing, then, primarily because it acts as a bell or siren telling you it's time to take notice, it's time to do something, to make a change, to cope, or adapt. That your body is equipped to "feel" stress is remarkable; our job is to use the signals our bodies send out to alert us to the stage of stress it's in, and do something about the level of stress our body is experiencing. Here's what you should know about the nature of stress so that you can do just that.

"Fight or Flight": The "Alarm Phase" of Stress

This first phase of stress alerts the body to the stressful encounter—warning it that it's time to make what we call a "fight-or-flight" response. In other words, the body gears up to take action. In stressful situations, messages from the brain trigger an outpouring of adrenaline from the adrenal glands. Circulation speeds up, more energy-rich sugar appears in the blood, muscles tense, saliva decreases, eyes dilate, senses become more acute, the thyroid is activated and the body's muscle function is strengthened. At the same time, blood cells are released from storage depots into the circulation, and the digestive system goes into temporary inaction. All of these reactions are designed to help the body gear up for action. You may recognize some of the following alarm reaction responses from your own experience.

✓ Do you remember how your heart pounded when a speeding car wheeled around the corner, taking you by surprise and, luckily, just missed hitting you? In such situations, the heart speeds up and blood pressure soars, forcing blood to parts of your body that need it, thus carrying oxygen-rich blood to organs so they will be instantly fueled for action— including the brain, so it can make wise decisions quickly!

✓ Can you remember trying to catch your breath after being frightened (like the time you were concentrating on an assignment or project and the wind caused the door to slam shut)? This reaction is caused by breathing faster to supply more oxygen for the needed muscles.

✓ Remember getting your "second wind" the time your best friend was involved in a confrontation and you rushed over to help? Or were you once surprised by your strength and endurance during an emergency when you could tell from your dog's yelp that your pet might need your help? The extra strength came from sugars and fats pouring into your bloodstream to provide fuel for quick energy.

✓ Do you use extra deodorant when you know you're going to be under pressure, like going in to interview for a part-time job that you really want to get, or asking someone special for a date when you are unsure if he or she will accept? You perspire more when under stress. This is because perspiring is how the body tries to cool down. The cooler your body, the more efficient its energy.

✓ Do you ever have a stiff neck after a long test or a really stressful day? In high-stress situations, muscles remain in a state of tenseness. Strained muscles are sore muscles.

✓ Have you ever had "knots" or "butterflies"—or "eagles"!— in your stomach before taking an exam or making a presentation in front of your classmates? Because it's more important to be alert and strong in the face of danger than to digest food, your digestion slows so blood can be directed to your muscles and brain.

"The Coast is Clear!": The "Resistance/Adaptation Phase" of Stress

Almost immediately following a stressful event, the body attempts to return to its normal balance. We call returning to "normal" homeostasis, a state of calm and normal functioning. In this phase, the body works to reverse the process described in the alarm stage, but only if it believes that the stressful encounter is over. If the danger is over, the body works to restore a state of calm by lowering blood pressure, heart rate, respiration and core body temperature. But if your body senses that danger is still present—you are still greatly worried or frightened—then the body replaces its temporary and emergency responses with more fixed ones. Muscle tension is a good example of this kind of "replacement" response. This is not a good thing because a great deal of energy and body nutrients (such as potassium and vitamin B) are depleted. Such nutrients are needed to not only keep you healthy, but also to help you fend off stress.

Here's how this works: Let's say, for example, you are home alone and hear a strange creaky noise in your house. This noise frightens you. Always working for you, your body gears up— your senses become keen, and your eyesight is sharpened—just in case you need to confront or flee the scene. Let's assume for a moment that the creaking noise continues every few minutes for the next couple of hours, making you so frightened that you decide to turn the lights on all over the house. You even go to your room, push your dresser in front of the door and sit quietly, your lamp in your hand in case the now larger-than-life "monster" decides to come down your hallway!

But now let's assume that while sitting in your room, you look up and discover that outdoors, the wind is blowing so strong that even the lamps in the street are swaying. Feeling relieved, you conclude that the creaking is obviously caused by strong winds—and this dispels the notion of anything sinister. Maybe you even laugh at the situation. For the rest of the evening, even though the creaking noise continues, you are no longer fearful. Having this information that you are safe, your brain triggers the "coast is clear" message, and your body returns to homeostasis, a state of relaxed normal.

But now let's assume that you never really are sure what is causing that frightening noise. If that were the case, you would remain in a heightened state of arousal—because of being fearful—and your body would stay in a state of tense alert. This is when the body moves to the third phase, the exhaustion phase.

"Burnout": The "Exhaustion Phase" of Stress

When your body is under a period of prolonged and intense stress, it gets exhausted. Sometimes this is referred to as "burnout." Do you feel drained after a big test? What if the test went on for three weeks? You can only imagine how exhausting that would be. This same sort of wear and tear happens when you are constantly worried about something, even something that slowly brews—such as worrying about if your parents will get back together if they are separated, or if someone will find out that it was you who started a particular rumor or whether everything will go perfectly for your big party.

Prolonged stress can be dangerous over time because when you are under stress, your body uses your reserve of essential vitamins and minerals. Staying under stress for a long time means that these essential nutrients are drained from your body, and so your ability to withstand stress is lowered. If you are under stress for a long time (experts place this time period as anywhere from three weeks to three months), your supply of energy is used up, leaving you at risk for harming your bodily organs.

Since mind and body work in unison, when your body is tired, so is your emotional state of mind. One teen summed it up well when she said, "I was so exhausted from the constant stress I felt when my parents were divorcing that I reached a point where I felt drained and unable to 'get up' for my own school and personal life."

When you are in the midst of a long period of stress in your life, it's especially important to take care of yourself. Getting enough rest, eating the essential high-quality foods to restore your body and making sure you take the time to get the exercise your body needs to burn up excess stress, as well as relaxing the body so it can rejuvenate, are all very important steps to staying in good health.

VIRTUAL PRACTICE: YOU AND STRESS

Think of a time over the last few months when you experienced the **alarm phase** of stress. What was happening to cause the stress?

_____

_____

How did you know your body was alerting you it was in this phase of

stress? _____

_____

Think of a time over the last few months when you experienced the **resistance/adaptation phase** of stress. What was happening to cause this stress? _____

_____

How did you know your body was in this phase of stress?

_____

_____

Think of a time over the last few months when you experienced the **exhaustion phase** of stress. What was happening to cause you stress?

_____

_____

How did you know you were in this phase of stress and how did you get your energy back?

_____

_____

Cool is Up To You!

One of the benefits of understanding the nature of stress is so that you can learn to use it to your advantage. Just as stress can be debilitating (such as stopping you from thinking clearly), you can make it work in your favor. How can you use stress in a positive way rather than letting it get the best of you? Knowing the benefits of responding to a stressful situation in a positive manner is a start. In other words, you can learn to be cool under stress.

Speaking of cool, when you're stressed-out, how does your body respond? How do you feel? How do you behave? The next chapter will help you examine the three ways stress shows up in your life.

CHAPTER 3

The Three "Side Effects" of Stress: Physical, Emotional and Behavioral

While stress is a natural reaction of our body in response to the demands we make upon it, it's important that we always be aware of the amount of stress, strain and pressure we put ourselves through. Why? Because as you learned in the last chapter, too much stress can take a toll, and not just physically—such as feeling overwhelmed, burned out, or in an extreme case, by getting an ulcer or suffering other health breakdowns. Stress also affects the way we feel (emotions) and the ways in which we behave. Health experts confirm that "side effects" of stress are threefold: physical, emotional and behavioral. As you can see in the story below, the stress and strain seventeen-year-old Gerard Hamilton felt in his efforts to deal with "goddess" Cassandra affected him in all three ways!

The Trouble with a Goddess

Cassandra Allen is practically a goddess—she's that cool. What's more, she is smart and funny and beautiful and nice to everyone—even kids who aren't popular like her. I've been secretly in love with Cassandra for almost a whole semester now, and hoping there would come a time when I got the chance to ask her to go out with me. For the last two months she's been dating one of the most popular guys in school, Manny Ellison. Before that it was exchange student Jake Lidstrom, and before that, a "serious" relationship with Neil Garza. But she's done with all of them! So finally, I saw my chance. Cassandra wasn't dating anyone and wasn't even interested in anyone else (I got this on good authority from my younger sister, who got it from Cassandra's younger sister). Best of all, the Christmas formal was fast approaching and surely she would want a date to the Christmas formal. Not that Cassandra wouldn't be able to get any number of guys to ask her to go to the formal—like I said, she's a goddess.

When you ask out a girl like Cassandra, you have to plan things carefully, look for the right moment and say the right thing—because once you get a "no," you pretty much lose confidence to try again.

The "right moment" meant asking her when no one else was around. I did know her schedule and where her locker was located, so two weeks before the dance, I spent every spare school-hour minute watching for the time when she was alone so I could ask her.

All this was pretty exciting, but nerve-wracking, too. Still, I considered it well worth it. I'd spent hours practicing what I was going to say and how I was going to approach her. My plan was that once the time was right, I'd stop to say "Hello" as I was strolling by, then pull a pack of gum from the pocket of my shirt and offer her a piece (I thought that was a great touch: you know, just to make it all seem casual). Then I'd say: "Hey, Cassandra. What'cha up to? Want a piece of gum?" I'd be gallant as I handed her the stick of gum. She'd smile, I'd smile and then I'd say, "How would you like to go to the Christmas formal with me?" I'd practiced the words so they would have a warm but "no pressure" tone. (You don't want to make a goddess feel pressured.)

I must've rehearsed the scene in my head a hundred times. The problem was that right moment never presented itself. The wait was torture, and I was getting anxious: The Christmas formal was fast approaching. The stress of it all was really wearing. I found myself daydreaming in class, and not really concentrating on my studies. It even spilled over with my friends, as I discovered one day when Joel Burrows, one of my best friends, came up to me and asked if I'd go with him to the school library to help him check out a book he badly needed for his next class. Because he owed a late fee for a book, the librarian wouldn't let him check the book out under his own library card. Well, normally I'd just go do it for him, but from the corner of my eye, I'd just had a Cassandra-the-goddess sighting. She was out in the school courtyard—alone—just looking through her notebook. Thinking "now's the moment!" I was suddenly faced with my best friend needing an urgent favor. "You're always needing something!" (which isn't the case at all) I barked unfairly.

Joel looked surprised and kind of hurt. I looked up, and poof! Cassandra was gone. My friend left, too, and that upset me as well. By Wednesday I still hadn't seen her alone again, and by Thursday, I had a headache at the end of the school day, and my shoulders and neck were actually aching.

The next day, I finally got another chance: Cassandra was actually alone at her locker! How long would it last? My heart began to pound, my pulse was zipping along like hummingbird wings. I scanned the area—no one was approaching Cassandra in the distance—this was it! I set out on my practiced "stroll." When I got to Cassandra, just as rehearsed, I said, "Hello, Cassandra." Cassandra glanced at me and smiled, then continued digging in her locker, "Hi, Gerard. Gosh, I can't find my civics book!"

Remembering my props, I pulled my pack of gum from the pocket of my shirt and offered her a piece. Remembering my lines, I asked, "What'cha up to? Want a piece of gum?" I tried to be gallant as I handed her the stick of gum. She turned to look at me again, this time her expression baffled, as if wondering if I was deaf. "Gum?" she asked, then shook her head—whether in refusal of the gum or in wonder at my stupidity, I don't know. Then to my horror, I dropped the gum, so I was sweating—literally and obviously. I dove to the ground to pick up the gum and accidentally spilled the contents of my backpack—books crashed and pencils rolled.

Remembering how I'd once pictured Cassandra opening her mouth gracefully and placing the gum in it, instead her mouth was open all right—but in a kind of "is he for real?" expression. But miracles do happen, and to my amazement she stooped down to help me pick up my stuff. "Gerard, are you okay?" she asked? (I told you she was nice.) I sighed and confessed, "I wanted to look cool."

"You wanted to look cool?" she repeated and then laughed. "If you really want to be cool, why don't you ask me to the Christmas formal? I've been hoping you would, but I'm not going to wait for you much longer."

"Yeah. I mean yes. Sure. Great! Okay, then."

"Good," she said, "so let's talk about the details after school tomorrow. I've got squad practice tonight and tons of homework." It was that simple—all that worry, drama and disaster and in the end I got the answer I'd waited forever to hear. I wish I'd known that was how it was going to turn out before I made myself a nervous wreck. But that's the trouble with a goddess, you never know just what she's going to do—or say.

Gerard Hamilton, 17

How to Recognize the (Physical, Emotional and Behavioral) Signs and Symptoms of Stress

Gerard's dealings with a "goddess" make it clear that trying to get a date with a special someone can have some side effects (check out some of Gerard's symptoms in the following section). What causes these symptoms? Health experts have found that stress triggers chemical changes in the brain and alters the body's chemical balance, all of which has an effect on the way we think, act and feel. Depression, for example, has been associated with low levels of two neurotransmitters: serotonin and norepinephrine. These may be big words, but ask anyone who has ever been "blue," "in a funk" or "depressed," and they'll no doubt describe a time of intense stress.

Stress can result in muscle tension, headaches, stomachaches, feeling irritable, not being able to concentrate and even result in feelings of low self-worth. Here are some other common symptoms of stress.
Symptoms of Stress

- headaches
- continued feelings of being annoyed or irritated
- low energy or bouts of high energy
- dramatic change in food cravings
- feeling like a victim, feeling "trapped"
- outbursts of temper
- pains in the lower part of your back or neck or shoulders
- feeling "blue," or lonely
- lack of interest in things once enjoyed (such as time with friends)
- heart pounding or racing
- jumping from peaks to valleys of self-esteem
- nausea or upset stomach
- inferiority feelings
- sleep difficulties (too much/too little)
- difficulty making decisions
- loss of concentration
- feeling hopeless

A good way to look at the effects of stress is to break them into three distinct categories: physical, emotional and behavioral. Pinpointing these stress reactions is yet another clue for you in learning how to deal with the stress and strains in your life. For example, if you know you're going to get a tension headache just before taking a big test, using a quick muscle relaxation exercise can help you avoid some of the tension. Let's look at how Gerard said the incident with the "goddess" affected him.

Physically	Emotionally	Behaviorally
I got headaches.	I got nervous. (I'd often stutter.)	I didn't eat.
I lost my appetite.	I felt insecure.	I acted "love-sick."
My hands got shaky.	I was irritable.	I couldn't concentrate.
I began to sweat. My muscles tensed.	I felt scattered.	I was short-tempered.
My heart pounded.	I was hyper.	I snapped at my friends.
		I didn't meet all my responsibilities.

VIRTUAL PRACTICE:
HOW DOES STRESS AFFECT YOU?

How does stress affect you? Place a checkmark beside those that apply to you. Then, on the lines provided, list other ways stress exerts power over you.

The Physical Side Effects of Stress

How stress affects me *physically*:
- ❑ My muscles get tense.
- ❑ My hands get cold or sweaty.
- ❑ My stomach feels as if it is churning.
- ❑ I have difficulty sleeping.
- ❑ My heart beats rapidly.
- ❑ I have sudden bursts of energy.
- ❑ I am extremely tired.
- ❑ I lose my appetite, or eat too much.

- _____
- _____

The Emotional Side Effects of Stress

How stress affects me *emotionally*:
- ❑ I get nervous.
- ❑ I cry.
- ❑ I want to strike out or hit something.
- ❑ I feel sad.
- ❑ I giggle a lot.
- ❑ I worry excessively and can't stop thinking, "what if?
- ❑ I am irritable or feel depressed.
- ❑ I feel bad about myself.
- ❑ I daydream a lot at school.
- ❑ I get angry easily, even explosive.
- ❑ I lose interest in my appearance.

- _____
- _____

The Behavioral Side Effects of Stress

How stress affects my *behavior*:
- ❑ I have difficulty concentrating.
- ❑ I substitute food, drugs or alcohol for coping.
- ❑ I become grouchy, irritable, even mean.
- ❑ I cover up by not being honest about something.
- ❑ I get into arguments or fights with others.
- ❑ I deliberately do sloppy work (not caring about how it is done).
- ❑ I procrastinate.
- ❑ I smile a lot to cover up my feelings.
- ❑ I ignore my feelings.

- _____

- _____

Cool is Up To You!

While some amounts of stress can help us feel creative and move us to action, too much can cause us to feel overwhelmed, even debilitated. So, you'll want to know what you can do to use it to your advantage. That's why knowing how stress affects you physically, emotionally and behaviorally can be useful information.

Obviously, you can't make all the stress and pressures of life evaporate, nor should you ignore them. Coping effectively is the key. How do you cope when stress comes your way? In the following chapters, you'll get a chance to find out.

CHAPTER 4
How Do You [Re]Act When You're Stressed-Out?

When you're face-to-face with a stressful situation, how do you react? Are you cool and confident under stress, or does it change your demeanor from cool to ghoul? Think about that for a moment. Let's say you're in school, and you're moseying down the hall on your way to your last-period class. It's been a long day and you're tired, and this last class isn't necessarily your favorite subject. You just wish the school day was over and that you were on your way home. You have exactly fifty seconds to get to class—and experience tells you it'll take a full minute to get down the hall, turn left at the library, down that corridor, take a right at the science lab, and whew, finally you'll be there. The thing is, you have to get there on time; you simply cannot be late. Another tardy will surely take a toll; even with all your persuasion and charm, it won't work for you today because you've used up all the teacher's patience with your being late to class. You take off on a full run!

What are some of the possible results of the stress of feeling you'll be late? Possibility one: Panicked and consumed with thoughts of some of the most terrible outcomes of your being late to class—like getting a lowered grade after a certain amount of tardies (which, by being late today, you will most certainly qualify to be a recipient); like your parents not allowing you to use the car during the week if your grades drop; like not making the honor roll—you bump into a group of students in a huddle, causing one of them to drop the books and notebooks in her arms. Now having to help your classmate pick up her dropped things, and knowing this upset has sealed your fate on being late for class, you get even more frustrated—and consider skipping class altogether!

Possibility two: Having set your course to get straight to class and focused on each and every little detail, including steering clear of the students in the huddle (as well as slowing your speed to "power walk" as you pass the teacher standing outside his classroom talking with a student), your mad dash pays off. You arrive on time, albeit panting. Smiling ear to ear—and happy that the stress of the moment has stirred up enough of your body's endorphins to keep you awake during the class— you take your seat, beaming and energized to boot.

Of course, there are other ways this scenario could play out, but you get the idea! Here's the good news: You get to decide how you react. While a situation creating stress isn't always under your control, how you respond is.

So how do you act and react to stress? Are you overwhelmed by it, or instead, exhilarated by it?

There is no such thing as a stress-free life. Nor is it possible to stop, even change, some of the stressful times that come our way. If you have a huge test in the next class and you are simply not prepared, and are overtired from getting back late on the bus from your school game, you probably can't do too much about being tired and that test waiting for you. You'll have to do the best you can. So while you can't always change the stressor, you can focus on you and your reaction to the situation at hand. In this instance, for example, you can encourage yourself to do the best you can, and maybe even explain your situation to the teacher and see if he or she will allow you to take the test at another time. Maybe the teacher will allow this, and maybe he or she won't.

Managing yourself is an important concept in that if you don't intervene, things can get out of hand. Have you ever set up a row of dominoes, and then triggered them into falling? Stress can cause a similar effect in that one stressful event (when not stopped) can trigger and provoke the next stress reaction. While having one domino trigger a chain reaction might be good when it comes to the row of dominoes, it's not what you want to have happen in the face of stress, as fifteen-year-old Rob Lawson found out. Because his snooze alarm didn't go off one morning, he found himself in a landslide of stress. Let's check in with Rob to find out why his stress dominoed its way from running late to running rampant.

You Snooze, You Lose!

I set my alarm for seven o'clock in the morning, but when it went off, I hit the snooze button, thinking I'd catch five more minutes of sleep. Well, the snooze alarm didn't go off!

When I looked over and saw that it was 7:45, I couldn't believe it! I skipped breakfast so I could run to catch the bus, but I missed it anyway. Luckily, my father hadn't left for work yet, so I asked him for a ride to school. He wasn't too happy about it because it meant he would be late for an appointment. We rode to school in silence.

By the time I got to school, the five-minute bell had already rung, so I had to go to the office to get a late pass. I hadn't asked my father to write a note for my being late, so I sat out first hour in the principal's office. By now, things were really starting to snowball. Since I was absent from my first-hour class, I missed my science test. My teacher said I couldn't make up the test since I had an unexcused absence. When

I went to my locker to get my books for my second-hour class, my math book was missing. My locker-mate, Barney Johnson, had picked up my book instead of his own. I was frantic. I hadn't turned in my math assignment the day before, and Mr. Cohen warned me not to let it happen again. My overdue math paper was in the book Barney had, and I had no idea where he could be, so, rather than face the teacher, I decided to skip math class! The math teacher took attendance, and because I wasn't reported on the absence list the vice-principal called my mother at work to tell her that I wasn't in school. When I got to third-hour class, my friends teased me about my whereabouts during second hour. I was in no mood for their humor. "Why don't you just worry about yourself?" I snapped, "Who do you think you are, a truant officer?" Being upset with my friends always makes me feel bad.

Standing in the lunch line, I noticed Barney Johnson. "Hey, Johnson! You took my math book, you idiot!" I called out. Barney yelled back, "Get off my back, you jerk!" At the end of my rope, I shoved Barney against the wall, my fist raised ready to hit him, when who should appear but the vice-principal! Surprised to see me, he ordered me to get away from Barney, informed me about the call he made earlier to my mother and took me to the office. Knowing my mother had been told that I wasn't in school made me feel even more stressed out. I knew she was going to call my father and tell him, too. Since I wasn't allowed to leave the office because I was in trouble for fighting, I wasn't able to make a call from the hall pay phone, either.

Finally, the school day was over. What a nightmare. And I still had to face my parents! I learned the hard way that when you snooze, you lose.

Rob Lawson, 15

What to Do When Stress Takes Over

As Rob found out, when one event collides and crashes into the next, your stress begins to resemble dominoes tumbling. Instead of letting your stress snowball to a point where it's controlling you, try to control your stress. Here are three important things to do.

1. **Admit you're out of control.** Don't collide from one reaction to the next, trying to deny that you're not feeling out of control—or trying to pretend that nothing is wrong.
2. **Decide to get back in control.** Make a decision to regroup and look for the solution. Stop and gain a new perspective, then commit to a better course of action.
3. **Deal with the stress going on in this moment.** Look for the next indicated step and then take it. Don't project and worry

about those stressors you'll be facing in the future; stay in the here and now and do what you have to do.

VIRTUAL PRACTICE: STOPPING THE CYCLE OF STRESS

Think about a time when something similar to Rob Lawson's experience happened to you, when the "cycle of stress" was under way and rolling out of control.

- At what point did you know your stress was "out of control"?

- What did you do?

- Who did you turn to for help and support? What did you ask of that person?

- What do you think you could have done differently so that things wouldn't have become as stressful?

- At what point could you have "rescued" things for yourself, and thus gotten back in control?

- What "price" did you pay for being out of control? For example, did it land you in trouble with anyone? If so, with whom?

- What did you do to get yourself back on track? What did you learn as a result, and how can you use this information the next time you feel out of control?

Cool is Up To You!

Understanding how one event leads to another is an important step in getting back in control when things begin to spin out of control. This is also important information for you in knowing what to do, and when. And of course, putting in place those skills that help you "regroup" sends a message to you (and others) that you are learning to manage yourself in stressful situations, and seeing yourself as capable in managing yourself in relation to stress.

Building a storehouse of positive experiences helps you face other stressful situations with confidence.

CHAPTER 5
Do You "Thrive" on Stress?

Not all people shy away from stress; some welcome it! How about you? Do you feel like the more intensity in situations, the better? Do challenges like a deadline or a jam-packed schedule gear you up for action? Do you like "extreme edge" events such as in-line skating, kick boxing or bike racing? Are you excited by goals, motivated by stress?

If you like the thrill of "edge events," you may be what experts in the field of stress refer to as a "stress-seeker." Certainly this is a trait that holds true for *National Geographic's* Boyd Matson—and fifteen-year-old Joshua Thomas (in the story below), who would like to follow in his footsteps—literally. Joshua is definitely looking forward to some adventurous, and stressful, times!

Globe-Trotting, Jungle-Braving, Tundra-Probing—Boyd Matson!

When I grow up I hope to be like the globe-trotting, jungle-braving, tundra-probing Boyd Matson! As the host of *National Geographic Explorer*, Boyd Matson's whole life is like one big adventure after another—and he gets paid a lot of money for it!

Just look at all the wild animals he gets to play with: snakes, bears, bats, mountain lions, chimpanzees. And his job includes traveling everywhere in the world—the Sahara Desert, Chile, New Zealand, Patagonia, the Sierra Nevada Mountains, the Amazon, New Guinea, the Arctic. My very greatest hope is to travel like that when I grow up. Everywhere he goes is an adventure. He went cave-diving in underwater caverns in Wakulla Springs, Florida, and climbed Africa's highest mountain, Mount Kilimanjaro in Tanzania. In the Dominican Republic, he swam with humpback whales. In Hawaii, he stood on the rim of the active Kilauea volcano.

He's always facing extreme-edge, thrilling adventure—like the time he hand-fed sharks in the Bahamas, or the time he was charged by hippos and elephants in Botswana. Once he actually rappelled into the Devil's Sinkhole in Texas, which is filled with six million bats. He's even journeyed across the outback in Australia with no food or water. All the things he gets to do are so cool.

Besides having all that fun and excitement, Boyd Matson also gets to help the planet in a lot of ways, such as helping biologists tag polar bears in the wild, piloting the Sustainable Seas Expedition's experimental one-person submarine, and joining crews from around the country to fight wildfires in Florida.

Imagine living a life of adventure, traveling all over the world while doing an important job that's a real taste berry to the planet— just like Boyd Matson. It's exactly what I hope for out of life!

Joshua Thomas, 15

Extreme Edge: The *Thrill* of Stress!

Stress-seekers thrive on pressure, competition and risk. These are the individuals who say they do their best when "under the gun." In fact, they sometimes wait until the last minute so as to create a deadline—because they like the "now or never" intensity. Rather than being overwhelmed by stress, they are motivated by it. They may even drift through a project halfheartedly if they start far ahead of time, not putting their focused all-and-all into it. But, knowing "this is it" compels them to apply themselves. While doing things in this way creates a lot of stress for some people, for others a stress-filled agenda is an atmosphere that helps them feel alive and inspired and that motivates them into action.

Are you a stress-seeker? The following quiz will help you know for sure.

VIRTUAL PRACTICE: ARE YOU A STRESS-SEEKER?

The following checklist will help you see if you are someone who thrives on stress. Read each of the statements and then using a rating of 1 to 4 (4 = Always; 3 = Frequently; 2 = Sometimes; and 1 = Never) rate yourself as to how you typically react in each situation.

_____ 1. Do you tend to put things off until the last minute and then have to "bear down" to get them done?

_____ 2. Are you "at home" or comfortable in those situations where there's pressure, competition or risk?

_____ 3. Have deadlines or competition been a driving force behind many of your accomplishments?

_____ 4. Do you feel exhilarated or energized while working toward a difficult task or reaching a big goal?

_____ 5. Do you enjoy being in situations that are new, unfamiliar or different from what you're used to?

_____ 6. Do you tend to see obstacles as challenges rather than headaches?

_____ 7. Are you constantly looking for ways to improve yourself, such as to get better grades or to improve your performance in sports?

_____ 8. Do you prefer friends who are risk-takers rather than those who "play it safe"?

_____ 9. Do you often compete, challenge or make a bet with yourself?

_____ 10. Do you like to "come down" or "calm down" shortly after a tension-producing event?

_____ 11. When you're looking for things to do, like planning your weekends and having your "vote" in where and what will be done for family vacations, do you suggest activities that include a lot of action?

_____ 12. Do you like activities that include a certain amount of competition or risk (for example, activities like rock climbing, racing or dirt-bike jumping)?

What Does Your "Score" Mean?

What does your total score mean? If your score is between 36 and 48, you are a stress-seeker who enjoys excitement and exhilaration. You actually look around for and create a high-stress level to propel you to action. You like stress. You thrive on it!

If your score is between 24 and 35, you probably like things to go smoothly; you like harmony and strive to keep things in perspective, to balance your life in order to stay on an even keel. A score between 12 and 23 indicates that you are likely to avoid stress and seek security instead. You prefer not to be charged with emotion and find such conditions drain and sap your energy.

Is being a stress-seeker a negative or positive? Actually, it is neither. Being a stress-seeker is a part of your personality. And of course, if you are stress-seeker who finds the stress you are looking for, hopefully you can also deal with it. What could be more stressful than attracting stress but then not using this "tempo" to your benefit? Likewise, if you are someone who likes things smooth, easy and trouble-free, that's not a negative either. It's just the way you prefer it. So what's the benefit in knowing if you are a stress-seeker? When you know you are stress-seeker you can then accommodate it! If you wait for the last minute to get things done, for example, then when it's time to "bear down" get to it!

Cool is Up To You!

Stress can be exciting! Certainly the person who is a stress-seeker uses it as a motivator. Being motivated and successful in meeting the challenges of stress is what keeps stress in check—which prevents it from snowballing into a landslide of stress. The good news is that while you can't always prevent stress, you can manage yourself in relation to it.

In this next chapter, you'll meet two teens who find themselves in a similar situation—each one handling things differently. It's a very good example showing how stress can get the best of you, or, how to be cool even when you're "locked out."

CHAPTER 6
Stress: Cool or Ghoul—is Up To YOU!

Our friends Sherry and Monica have similar personalities, yet they react so differently in stressful situations. For example, both girls are usually very shy and reserved. Yet when Sherry is "stressed to the max" she gets really quiet and even withdraws from wanting to be around others. On the other hand, when Monica is stressed-out, she moves out of her shyness and lets you know about it—often getting edgy, irritable and even loud. As with most of us, how we respond to stress is an individual matter, as you'll see as you read about a stressful experience that happened to two teens in Tacoma, Washington—Leah Matheson and Karen Billings. Both eleventh-graders arrive at school early one morning. Pulling into the parking space for students, Karen spots her good friend, Tina Bruner. The girls get out of their cars, call out hellos and walk to the school building together, talking about their plans for the weekend.

A few minutes later, Leah Matheson arrives in the same parking lot, hoping to get to the library as quickly as she can so that she can look up a reference book. She has an important test in Mrs. Willit's class this morning, and hopes to do well on it. Leah is quite sure the test will contain questions from a particular chapter in the reference book, and she wants to review the chapter. Leah hurries into the building, makes several quick stops and then heads for the library. Meanwhile, Karen goes along with her friend, Tina, to her locker, and after Tina gets the books she needs, the girls head off to Karen's locker to retrieve the books she'll need. That's when Karen realizes that in her hurry to get to school, she's forgotten her backpack! About this time, Leah finds the reference book she is looking for, sits down at a table and reaches into her backpack with the intention of reviewing some of her class notes centering around the reference book. She searches through her papers, but cannot find the notes. Then she realizes that when she packed her backpack this morning, she forgot to pick up the study notes, which she'd laid on her bathroom sink so she could review them while she brushed her teeth.

Since each girl lives close to school and has ample time to return home, pick up the items she needs and still make it back to school without being late—each makes the decision to return home to get what she needs. Small problem: Neither girl can locate her keys! But even though each girl faces the same problem, each one responds differently to the situation—the stressor. As is the case with stress, each girl's response to the situation at hand determines the stress level she feels. But let's have them tell their own story.

Not Two of a Kind

Leah Matheson: "While still in the library, I reached into my purse to retrieve the keys, only to discover they weren't there. Discovering they were gone, I frantically raced around, asking all my friends if they had seen my keys. 'Nope,' they all replied calmly, and then went on with their business—as if a major crisis wasn't at hand! Their calmness only added to my frustration. I ran around searching every inch of where I'd been, looking wildly in every room I'd been in—the rest room, the library (I looked on every bookshelf twice!) the rest room yet again. Then, I stormed to my locker and pulled everything out of it, recklessly tossing out every single item, shaking out the books (as if a set of keys could be slipped inside of them). I'm sure I looked like a total madwoman.

"Next, remembering that I had bought some juice from the hall snack dispenser, I actually clawed through the trash can, thinking I might have accidentally thrown my keys away along with the juice carton and napkin. They weren't there—and by this time I know that I looked 'trashed.' And so much time had gone by that even if I did find my keys, I'd never be able to make it home and back in time for my first-hour class. Totally frustrated, I headed for my class. Unable to even think of anything other than locating the keys, I forgot to get the books I needed from my locker before my next class, even after having spent all that time pulling it apart. Not only did I feel unprepared for the test the next hour, because I was so upset and scattered, I couldn't concentrate and just knew I'd do poorly (and the next day when the test grades were posted, my worst fears were realized).

"My stress showed in other ways, too. That morning, and for the rest of the day, too, I was demanding and impatient with my best friend, totally resenting that she would rather stand in the back hall in a lip-lock with her boyfriend than help me, her frantic friend, search the garbage for my keys. Then I was a grouch to my teachers because I was so worried about my keys and wished that I was looking for my keys instead of sitting in class. I ended up getting a headache and a nauseous feeling in my stomach. My whole day was shot."

Karen Billings: "When I noticed my keys were missing, something I'd gone through before, the first thing I did was to remind myself not to get too "nuts." I always lose my cool when I get that way, so

I decided instead to spend my energy finding my keys. I retraced my steps, considering the most likely place they could be. I told myself what I knew to be true—it would all work out one way or another. I'm not saying I didn't feel any stress—I just put my stress to work honing in on finding my keys. After checking every possible place they could be, I returned to my car to see if by chance the keys were still in the ignition. They were. But now there was a new problem: The car doors were locked!

"Now that I knew where the keys were, I started thinking of all the ways I could solve the problem. It seemed to me that the best way to resolve my dilemma was to call my mom at work to see if she could bring me an extra set of car keys over the noon hour. While I was a little disappointed that I'd be using my lunch hour to retrieve them (especially since I had planned on sitting with friends in the cafeteria for lunch), I didn't totally freak out. Though I regretted the inconvenience that it would cause my mom (and how it would interrupt her noon-hour plans), I didn't become upset. And I didn't run around looking like a buffoon. I went to first-hour class, made the necessary apologies for not having an important assignment turned in on time, and rather than make excuses for myself, told the teacher what had happened. It's not the greatest thing to get by for a half-day without your backpack when your homework and books are inside of it, not to mention my note to my boyfriend and my lip gloss, but it's not the end of the world. I had to explain to my teachers in the classes where I had homework assignments that were in the backpack; probably because I was honest and sincere about it, they gave me a break and let me bring my homework in the next day. The good news is that even though my free time with friends over lunch may have been shot, my whole day wasn't."

VIRTUAL PRACTICE:
YOUR REACTION TO STRESS IS UP TO YOU

While two individuals may experience the same stressful situation—such as accidentally locking their keys in their cars—the choice of how to respond is an individual one. Leah and Karen's different responses to the stressful situation of needing their homework and backpacks—and the keys to their cars to be able to get the things they needed—illustrates an important point: It was their responses to their situation—and not the situation itself—that determined how much stress each experienced.

And even Karen, who responded with relative calm, admitted, "I've locked my keys in the my car before. I panicked, ran around like a chicken with my head cut off, and basically stressed myself out to the point of having a bad day for the rest of the day. I know I looked as if I had the words 'Stressed-Out!' stamped on my forehead. And I'm sure my friends were just waiting for steam to come out of my ears! But I don't act like that anymore. I've discovered that my being stressed-out doesn't help me resolve my situation any sooner and, if anything, it makes it worse."

How do you respond to a stressful event? Do you get frustrated and go into a whirlwind of panic-stricken and futile activity? Or, do you use your stress as a call to action, as a sign to get busy and resolve the problem at hand?

The goal is for you to think about your typical reaction to a stressful event. Let's say you've left an important assignment at home and there is positively no way the teacher is going to let you off the hook for not producing it. You're standing outside the classroom, having just discovered your "problem." How would you respond to the situation at hand? Situations like these can show you how you handle stress. Again, in this book, we will show you some skills that can help you manage stress in efficient and effective ways.

Cool is Up To You!

As seventeen-year-old Kelly Anne Warren from Corvallis, Oregon, said, "Figuring out I didn't have to let everything 'get to me' was a real breakthrough—and a huge relief!" Sounds like Kelly Anne has learned that each of us gets to choose—at least to a large degree—how we're going to react in times of stress.

The following chapters will help you learn some important skills that can help you stay cool and think your way through a stressful situation. And you know how important it is to be cool!

CHAPTER 7

Coping Skills: The A + B = C Test
for Clear Thinking

Throughout this book you'll learn a good number of skills to help you manage stress as you make your way through stressful situations, including focusing on how to "think" your way through stressful times. In the workshops we conduct for teens on managing the stress, strains and pressures of teen life, many of you began to fondly refer to these skills as "noggin skills," a term we've since adopted. We'll help you use your "noggin" to think your way through stress—such as when you see that you're heading for a collision course and you know it's in your best interest to redirect the stress at hand to not make things worse.

Sixteen-year-old Jon Branson, had finally talked his mother into letting him ride to school with his best friend. One morning when riding to school with his buddy, Paul, he agreed to go with him to "check out the girls at Madison High." As destiny would have it, there he met a girl and soon his jaunts to Madison High were regular occurrences—as were his late arrivals to his own school! The jam he got himself into resulted in a lot of stress.

When stress closes in on you, it can be a good time to practice *the A + B = C Test for clear thinking.* This "slow down, let's think about what's happening" basic thinking skill helps you look squarely at what's going on, and then choose a response that's going to produce the best results. This way, you're sure to stay calm and cool under pressure, work your way out of the stress you're in and not create even more stress for yourself.

As for Jon, he's in a big mess, and his best bet is to think clearly and not dig himself in deeper trouble than he already is in. If he doesn't, his "Destiny" may just be fated for a new beginning elsewhere!

A Date with Destiny

I just knew when my friend Paul got his car, we'd be even better friends than we already were. When you've got a car, practically everyone wants to be your friend, but Paul and I have a lot in common, so I'm his best buddy. I started doing everything around the house and yard Mom asked me to do, because I planned to ask her if I could start riding to school with Paul.

Mom said, "No problem, as long as you get to school on time and riding with Paul doesn't distract you from being a good student."

Riding to school whith Paul, not my mother, made me feel like I was growing up! But I would have never guessed that Paul getting that shiny old Cougar would deliver me into what poets call "a date with destiny"! It all started one morning when Paul arrived and off we went to Madison High. "Hey, there's Jessica Waite!" Paul called and tapped on his horn, rolling down his window so Jessica could see him. Jessica smiled and waved back, said something to the two girls she was with and they came over to the car.

"Is this your car?" Jessica asked, and Paul nodded a proud, "Yep."

"Cool," Jessica complimented, then introduced us to Patty and then Destiny. I casually reached out a hand and said "hi" to Patty. I was about to do the same with Destiny when my eyes met hers—large green eyes, like pools of turquoise. They were soooo mysterious—as if I could swim into them. For me, it was love at first sight!

A guy doesn't really know what it is until it happens to him, nor is such a thing easy to describe—other than it feels as though you've been hit over the head with a tree; you're that sure that it's love. "Hi, Destiny," I said, my voice hardly sounding like my own. I was in total awe of her. To make a long story short, Paul and I zoomed off to Madison High every morning for the next two weeks. Needless to say, I was late to school each time.

Jon Branson, 16

Stress Affects Your Destiny, Too!

Jon's not getting to school on time is going to create a date with a destiny of a different nature—like with the attendance clerk at his school for being late, and answering to his mother for breaking his promise with her to get to school on time. Jon has some explaining to do—and this would be a good time to think clearly and rationally.

With stress closing in on his heels, it's a good time for him to practice the A + B = C Test for Clear Thinking. If Jon doesn't get things straightened out and on track, he is likely to find himself riding to school with his mother again. (And since it's highly unlikely his mom is going to swing by Madison High in the mornings, his "Destiny" may be looking for another guy!)

Thinking Clearly—and Logically—Can Help You Stay Calm and Cool Under Pressure (and Maybe Even Out of Trouble!)

There is a direct relationship between what you think and what you're likely to do as a result (your behavior). And how you respond (or react) to an incident sets the tone for what happens next, which can affect whether or not your stress goes away (or at least is minimized)—or whether it snowballs into even more stress. You can think of this chain of related events as the A + B = C effect.

> *A (your thinking) + B (your behavior)*
> *= C (the probable outcome of the situation).*

Keeping in mind that what you think determines your behavior—which can influence what happens next—let's check in on Jon to watch this formula in action as he faces up to one of the consequences of his being late to school: answering to his mother.

Incident: Jon's mom issues a consequence:
Jon's mother: "Jon, I know how much you like going to school with your friend Paul. When you asked me if you could ride with him, you assured me you wouldn't be late to school. However, the school called me because you've been late. Starting tomorrow, you'll need to start riding to school with me again."

Jon thinks about what's been said. There are any number of ways he could respond. Here are two possibilities.

A-1: Jon's irrational thinking:
"Mom knows how much I'd rather ride to school with Paul than with her. If she cared about whether or not I was popular with my friends, she would let me ride to school with Paul. She's not being fair. I wish she'd get off my back."

A-2: Jon's rational thinking:
"I wish I had kept a better handle on getting to school on time. I knew getting to school late would have consequences. And, I promised my mom I'd get to school on time when riding with Paul, and I didn't live up to my word. I'm disappointed in myself for not getting to school on time."

The "B" part of this equation is:

> *What you're thinking influences how you're likely to respond—your behavior.*

Let's look at how Jon's thinking influences his behavior in each example:

A-1: Jon's irrational thinking:
"Mom knows how much I'd rather ride to school with Paul than with her. If she cared about whether or not I was popular with my friends, she would let me ride to school with Paul. She's not being fair. I wish she'd get off my back."

B-1: Jon's rational behavior:
Glaring at his mother Jon accuses, "You're not fair! I have no life of my own, and now all my friends will think I'm a geek and it's because of you." He storms off to his bedroom, slamming the door behind him.

Thinking that it's his mother who is responsible for keeping him from riding to school with Paul, Jon decides to be upset with her and feels angry. This is not clear (or logical) thinking. If anything, he should be upset with himself for failing to live up to his end of the bargain to get to school on time. Instead, his feelings of being upset are focused on his mother. Yet it is Jon who is responsible: He didn't live up to the requirements (getting to school on time) to ride to school with his friend Paul.

Let's look at how this plays out when Jon thinks clearly and logically.

A-2: Jon's irrational thinking:
"I wish I had kept a better handle on getting to school on time. I knew getting to school late would have consequences. And, I promised my mom I'd get to school on time when riding with Paul, and I didn't live up to my word. I'm disappointed in myself for not getting to school on time."

B-2: Jon's irational behavior:
Owning his mistake, Jon then apologizes to his mother: "Mom, I know I promised I'd get to school on time, and it's my responsibility to do that. I'm sorry. I really want you to trust me and to feel that I'm mature enough to ride with my friend and still be to school on time. I hope that you'll give me another chance to prove that I can."

The "C" part of the equation is:

> *Your* behavior *is highly likely to influence the probable outcome of the situation.*

Jon's storming out of the room, for example, probably isn't going to work in his favor, and quite possibly will produce even more stress for him!

B-1: Jon's irrational behavior:
Glaring at his mother Jon accuses, "You're not fair! I have no life of my own, and now all my friends will think I'm a geek and it's because of you." He then storms off to his bedroom, slamming the door behind him.

C-1: Probable outcomes:
- Jon must ride to school with his mother instead of his friend.
- Jon is placed on phone restriction, and told he cannot call Destiny.
- The school places Jon on restriction for his tardiness.

See what happens when Jon is thinking clearly and logically.

B-2: Jon's rational behavior:
Owning his mistake, Jon apologizes to his mother: "Mom, I know I promised I'd get to school on time and it's my responsibility to do that. I'm sorry. I really want you to trust me and to feel that I'm mature enough to ride with my friend to school and still get there on time. I hope that you'll give me another chance to prove that I can ride with my friend and still be to school on time."

C-2: Probable outcomes:
- Jon's mother is proud to see Jon take responsibility for his actions and compliments him for owning his actions.
- Jon's mother tells him he must ride with her for the next two weeks and will evaluate it then.
- Jon's mother allows him to keep his phone privileges.

Will Jon Pass the "A + B = C" Clear Thinking Test?

When Jon's *thinking* about having to ride with his mother isn't clear, logical or rational, it works against him. He feels persecuted, upset and resentful. There are bound to be stressful ramifications for talking to his mother disrespectfully and storming from the room (which quite probably created even more stress for him). That Jon is thinking clearly and logically will reduce the stress at hand.

We're betting that Jon's mother accepts his apology and, being proud of him for taking responsibility for his actions, tells Jon he has one more chance to prove he can ride with his friend Paul and still get to school on time!

VIRTUAL PRACTICE: SKILLS TO SHARPEN YOUR THINKING CLARITY

Think about a stressful situation you're currently facing, and using the A + B = C process, work it through using the A + B = C process.

Cool is Up To You!

Thinking clearly reduces not only the stress of the moment, but also reduces the possibility that you'll behave in ways that will create even more stress for yourself. In the next chapter, we'll examine how you can look on the bright side of things, even if it's your nature to see the glass half-empty—a sure-fire way to get yourself on everyone's list of cool!

CHAPTER 8

Coping Skills: How to Be a Positive Thinker

Understanding that your thinking has an immediate bearing on the way you're likely to respond to an incident at hand is an important first step in managing stress. The choice is literally yours: As the old saying goes, "You can see the cup half-full or half-empty." In other words, just as you can convince yourself that things are "doom and gloom," so can you convince yourself that things will turn out in a beneficial way. How? Make a decision to see life from the cup-half-full point of view.

The Night the Power Went Out

My parents were in a huge argument, and I was really hurt and upset about it. I didn't know who I should talk with about how I was feeling, because for one, I didn't want any of my friends to find out how bummed-out I was. So while talking on the phone to my best friend Nikki, I started crying. When she asked me why I was crying, I told her I was just stressed-out about school stuff. "Hey, why don't you ask your mom if you can come over to my house and stay the night?" (She only lives three blocks from my house.) Though I knew I wouldn't tell her about my parents' situation, I was looking forward to just getting out of the house. So I asked my mom, and at first she said I could go. I was in the middle of packing up my schoolbooks and putting together an overnight case, when suddenly the power went out in our entire neighborhood.

Mom quickly got out some candles and, bringing one to my room, told me that because of the power, I couldn't stay with my friend. Then she told me that I needed to look in on my grandfather, tell him about the power going out, and stay with him in his room until it came back on. (Repairpersons were already working on restoring power.)

I was really disappointed about not being able to go to my friend's house, and not all that excited about now having to go sit with my grandfather who had recently moved in with us (because his health was frail and he could no longer care for himself alone). My grandfather is nearly eighty and, a very sweet man. But I knew he would be frightened alone, so I did as my mother asked.

I went to his room and informed him that the power had gone out in the neighborhood and that I'd stay until it had been restored. He seemed quite happy, and I assumed he was being his polite and sweet self. Then he said, "Great opportunity."

"What is?" I asked, not at all sure what he meant.

"To talk, you and I," he said. "To hold a private little meeting about what we're going to do with those two—your mom and dad, and my daughter and son-in-law. And what we're going to do with ourselves now that we're in the situation we're in."

"But we can't do anything about it, Grandpa," I said, surprised that here was someone with whom I could share my feelings—and with someone who was in the same "boat" as I was.

"Oh," he said, "we may not be able to talk sense into them, but we can talk about how we're going get through it, and we can help each other work through it. Do you think we can?"

And that's how the most incredible friendship between me and my grandfather started. Sitting there in the dark that night, we talked about our feelings and fears of life—from how fast things change, to how they sometimes don't change fast enough. We talked about so much. Not only did I come to know him better, but I discovered that Gramps would be my lifeline to comfort and soothe me when I felt overwhelmed. That night, in the dark, because the power had gone out, I'd found a new friend, a friend with whom I could safely talk about all my fears and pain, whatever they may be.

Suddenly, the lights all came back on. "Well," he said, "I guess that means you'll want to go now. I really liked our talk. I hope we can do it again. Maybe we'll get lucky and the power will go out every few nights!"

Jamie Dykes, 14

Seeing the Bright Side of Things
Can Help You Redirect Stress

Jamie and her grandfather turned that dark evening into brighter days ahead. Looking for the positive is a real asset when faced with a stressful situation. Try not to "make mountains out of molehills." It's easy to exaggerate feelings about the latest crisis. The thing is, while every molehill can look like a mountain, things aren't always as do-or-die as they first appear.

Was there ever a time when you were afraid to return a library book because it was *verrry* overdue? Did you really get into all that much trouble when you finally returned it? Did your parents stop loving you or your friends stop being your friends? Probably not. The key is to see that your worries and fears, while real, are not the end of the world.

Deciding that the world won't end is a real breakthrough.

Think about a big worry facing you right now. Now, imagine that it's one year later. How do you think you will feel about this problem in one year?

When it comes to skills for seeing the cup as half-full or for not making mountains out of molehills, a great place to begin is with the words you speak. It helps if you don't put yourself down by saying negative things about yourself. Doing so only makes you feel worse. Don't say things like "I'm so stupid," or "No one likes me," or "I just know I'm going to flunk that test!" These comments only bring you down in negative thinking and don't serve you well in getting to work on changing things. For example, if you tell yourself you are not a good student, you will probably find school stressful; this will contribute to your not liking school.

On the other hand, when you send mostly positive messages to yourself, you are more likely to influence things in a positive way. This is the first step in changing a poor situation to a more positive one. There is an expression that goes: When things are objectively bad, they may seem subjectively worse. This means things often seem worse than they are. A useful tool for coping with stressful situations is to remind yourself that there is light at the end of the tunnel. Tomorrow will come. You will be okay. Then, pick yourself up and coach your way through the stressful encounter.

Here are some helpful phrases for you to tell yourself to help you through stressful times. Read through each one of them and, in the space provided, add others that can support you in reducing stress.

Preparing for Everyday Stress:
For example, you are about to take an exam or to ask out a special someone, or you're running late getting to work after school.

Say to yourself:

- _Be calm. Just think about what I have to do. I need to put my energy towards that._
- _No negative self-statements. Just think rationally._
- _I'll just do my best and let go of the rest._

What else could you say?

- _____

Preparing for a Confrontation:

For example, you are about to face your parents or teachers about a promise you didn't keep, or you accidentally grabbed your locker-mate's book and you know she needed it and she's going to be upset with you.

Say to yourself:

- _This could be a rough situation, but I know how to deal with it._
- _I can work out a plan to handle this._
- _Keep your cool._

What else could you say?

- _____

Preparing to Meet a Big Challenge:

For example, you are going to take your test for your driver's license or it's the big day of your pep squad or basketball tryouts.

Say to yourself:

- _I can meet this challenge._
- _Relax. Take a slow deep breath._
- _There are a lot of wonderful things going on in my life; this is only one event, don't make it more than it is._

What else could you say?

- _____

Preparing to Cope with "Overwhelm":

For example, you are in the middle of a day that includes three final exams, and a job interview after school; or you're in charge of the prom committee and the big day arrives, and everyone is coming to you with questions on what to do and what goes where, and you still have to get it all done in time to get home and get dressed for the big event.

Say to yourself:

- _Take a deep breath and exhale slowly._
- _Focus on what is happening now; what is it I have to do._
- _I can make it through this._

What else could you say?

* _____

VIRTUAL PRACTICE: HOW TO CHANGE A NEGATIVE THOUGHT TO A POSITIVE ONE

Okay, you want to be a positive person, but there is this negative thought pestering you, trying to get the best of you. So how do you make it go away? You change it to a positive one. Changing or "rewriting" the way you think about something is a good way to stop focusing on the negatives and the "what ifs." Instead, focus on what you can do to change the situation in a positive way. How? By applying these three steps.

Step 1: Visualize a yellow stop sign whenever you start to get negative. In your mind's eye, make it big and yellow with the huge letters, STOP! This stop sign acts as a signal for you to stop thinking a negative thought and to replace it with a positive one.

Step 2: Reframe the thought, changing a negative thought to a positive one.

Step 3: Give yourself direction, one that points you toward a positive action.

EXAMPLE

Negative Thought: *"I don't have any friends."*

Reframe to a Positive Message: *"STOP! I do have friends. But though I'd like to be friends with Amber, she doesn't seem to want me as a friend. Still, Jenaye is a very good friend to me, and I have a lot of other friends, as well."*

Direction for Positive Action: *"I'm going to focus on being a good friend to my friends, and stay open and friendly with the goal of making even more friends."*

Your turn. What is a negative message you're in the habit of telling yourself? _____

_____

Reframe to a Positive Message: _____

_____

Direction for Positive Action: _____

_____

Cool is Up To You!

It takes a little practice, but you can change the way you think. Almost as quickly as that negative thought comes to mind, you can replace it with a positive one—and avoid all the stress that comes with negative thinking.

CHAPTER 9

Coping Skills: Quick and Easy Steps to Solve Problems

Have you ever been stressed-out making a decision, especially when the problem was so intense there didn't appear to be any solutions, as Sabrina is feeling?

Sonja and Sabrina—and Kyle Thurman!

My friend Sonja is a lot of fun. When she invited me to spend the night at her house on Friday, I really wanted to go. My parents can be strict about me being out overnight, so when I asked them if I could go, they had to know my exact plans, which included dinner and an at-home evening at Sonja's. Then, of course, they wanted to be sure that we would be "properly supervised" (my parents are big on that term). Well, I checked with Sonja, and she assured me that her mother was going to be there. After I passed this news along to my parents, they gave me permission.

That evening, my parents dropped me off and went on their way to have dinner with some friends. I waved good-bye to them and went to the front door. Sonja answered it with a huge grin. "You are not going to believe our good luck!" she screamed. "My mom is out of town at a trade show and she won't be home until tomorrow. So let's head to the movies. My brother said he'd drive us! Is that so cool?"

My parents and I had an agreement. I didn't want to break the trust I had with them, yet I really wanted Sonja to think I was cool; I also wanted to go to the movies. Besides being fun, Kyle Thurman was going to be there. Kyle is so cute and I've had a huge crush on him forever—every opportunity to even just glimpse him is golden.

I went from happily knocking on the front door to instant stress! What should I do? My parents were out with their friends, so I couldn't call and check with them about the new plans until much later in the evening. By then it would be way too late to go to the movies. If I went without their knowing, I'd be in big trouble. Yet, here was this perfect moment to be with Kyle Thurman, who is very popular. I was totally confused about what to do, and stressed to the max.

Sabrina van Arnem, 16

A 5-Step Approach to Solving Problems Effectively

Having a problem that you don't know what to do about is very frustrating, especially if you happen to act impulsively or make a rash decision, one that not only doesn't solve the problem but makes it worse. To solve a problem you have to identify the problem, search for sound solutions, try them out, then evaluate the consequences of your proposed solution.

Here's a simple but very effective five-step process to help you develop an organized approach to problem solving, one that involves asking yourself the following questions:

1. What is the problem?
2. How can I solve it?
3. What are the consequences?
4. What is my plan?
5. How did I do?

Here's the five-step problem-solving approach and how Sabrina used it to resolve her dilemma.

1. **What is the problem?** (Sometimes the problem is always readily apparent. If the problem is very complex, just keep asking yourself, "What else is the problem?") Here's what Sabrina identified as her problem:

    I accepted an invitation to an overnight stay based on certain criteria and assured my parents of these plans. Sonja has changed the plans without notifying me, and I can't locate my parents to get permission regarding the changes. Without their permission, I'm sure to be grounded. Trust me. But, Kyle— what an opportunity . . .

2. **How can I solve it?** (Here you should come up with as many possible ways you can think of to solve the problem; basically, this means asking, "What could I do to make the problem go away?") Here is how Sabrina worked through this part:

    Action #1: *I could go along with Sonja's new plans without telling my parents.*

Action #2: I could wait until my parents are home to contact them about getting permission to accept the new plans.

Action #3: I could tell Sonja that the new plans sound interesting but that I can't go, because I've told my parents one thing, and I'm certain they wouldn't approve of the new plans.

Action #4: I could tell Sonja that she's a poor friend to put me in this predicament.

Action #5: I could leave a message on my parents' answering machine, telling them of the change in plans, and go off to the movies—and be with Kyle!

3. **What are the consequences of each proposed solution (action)?** (Not all solutions work equally well. After you've generated as many possible solutions to the problem as you can, assess the potential outcome of each proposed action by asking, "If I do that, what would happen?" Thinking through potential outcomes can save you from experiencing even more stress!) Here is how Sabrina worked through this step:

Action #1: I could go along with Sonja's new plans without telling my parents.

Consequence #1: I'll break the trust me and my parents have established.

❦

Action #2: I could wait until my parents are home to contact them about getting permission to accept the new plans.

Consequence #2: It will be too late to go, and everyone will be in a bad mood from waiting for my decision.

❦

Action #3: I could tell Sonja that the new plans sound interesting but that I can't go, because I've told my parents one thing, and I'm certain they wouldn't approve of the new plans.

Consequence #3: I'll take the responsibility for my decision and run the risk that my friends will mock me.

❦

Action #4: I could tell Sonja that she's a poor friend to put me in this predicament.

Consequence #4: Sonja will feel offended, and it'll put a strain on our friendship.

❦

Action #5: I could leave a message on my parents' answering machine, telling them of the change in plans, and go off to the movies—and be with Kyle!

Consequence #5: My parents will most certainly feel taken advantage of and probably will say no to overnights in the future. Plus, I may be grounded for life!

4. **What is the plan?** (After considering all the consequences and which ones you are prepared to accept responsibility for, decide what you are going to do. Then, make a plan and commit to the plan.) Here's what Sabrina decided:

I'm going to tell Sonja that though the new plans sound interesting, I won't be able to accept them without first checking with my parents. I'll tell Sonja to go to the movies without me if she wants to, but that I don't want to take a chance on breaking the trust my parents have in me.

5. **How did I do?** (After you've followed through with your decision, evaluate how you did and make some value judgment about it. Was your decision a good one? What were the consequences of your decision?) Sabrina said this was the outcome of her decision:

I liked my decision. It worked. It helped me keep the faith with my parents. And, though I didn't know it at the time, as it turned out, my friend Sonja was relieved not to have to follow through with her own revised plans, knowing that her mother, too, would be upset when she learned of the incident.

VIRTUAL PRACTICE:
HOW TO BE A PROBLEM-SOLVING SLEUTH

Using the following situation, apply this five-step approach to deciding how to best solve the problem it presents. Helping Amy will help learn to use it in your own life.

Invited to the "Party of the Year"

Sixteen-year-old Amy gets invited to a big party at a senior's house, and all the upperclassmen will be there. "Great!" she thinks—until she realizes that party falls on the exact same day as her ten-year-old sister's birthday. Amy's family is taking her little sis, Margo, out to dinner with some of Margo's friends, and then coming back to the house for a surprise party, complete with birthday cake and presents. Amy's parents have asked her to be in charge of greeting guests and to "store them away" so that Margo is sure to be surprised. Amy definitely wants to be there for her little sister's surprise party—but not quite as much as she'd like to be at the upperclassman's party!

1. What is the problem? _____

    _____

2. How can Amy solve it?

    Action #1: _____

    _____

    Action #2: _____

    _____

    Action #3: _____

    _____

3. What are the consequences of each proposed solution?

    Action #1: _____

    _____

    Consequence #1: _____

    _____

    Action #2: _____

    _____

    Consequence #2: _____

    _____

    Action #3: _____

    _____

    Consequence #3: _____

    _____

4. What do you suggest Amy do? _____

    _____

5. If Amy follows your suggestion, how do you think things will turn out? _____

    _____

Cool is Up To You!

Having a plan to clarify and solve your problems is a great way to manage stress.

CHAPTER 10

Coping Skills: "Self-Talk"—How to Talk to Yourself When Stress Sets In

"Thinking out loud," commonly called "self-talk," can be used to guide yourself through a tense or difficult situation. It's a simple but sure way to focus your attention on what needs to be done this very minute. Rather than being "scattered" and "all over the map," you concentrate on the task at hand.

What should Brianna do for the big day when she'd like to help Romeo swoon?

Juliet—and Her Romeo

Ever since I heard about the drama club's upcoming production of Romeo and Juliet, I'd been rehearsing for the role of Juliet. More than anything I want to be an actress, a serious actress, and what's more serious than a leading part in Shakespeare? Every night, after all my homework was done, I'd get out the script, memorize lines and practice performing them in front of the mirror. I was in the middle of my best mirror-performance yet, when my mom came to my room to tell me that my friend Cassie was on the phone. Really excited, Cassie said, "You won't believe this! Todd Knowles is trying out for the role of Romeo!" Todd Knowles! Todd is the undisputed, positively the coolest guy in our school. Cassie knew I had a huge crush on Todd, and above all else in life I wanted to him to notice me.

"For sure?" I questioned.

"Yes, for sure," Cassie assured me. "I got it from his sister, Tara. But there's more. Didn't you say you were scheduled to read for Juliet right after school tomorrow? Welllll . . . that is the exact time that Todd is scheduled to read for Romeo, too. What that means is that you're going to read opposite Todd!"

My heart started racing—words failed me. I couldn't believe it. What if I got so nervous I'd forget my lines? He'd think I was dumb. And what if we did the kiss scene—tomorrow?

"Is this like too perfect? This is your big chance. Can you believe it?" Cassie gushed. "Of all the other guys reading for the role that you could've been scheduled to try out with, you get Todd Knowles. What luck!"

Of course, I was thrilled . . . I really was . . . but I'd been preparing to get the role for a play that would begin rehearsals in two weeks—however, I hadn't been preparing to actually read with and maybe even kiss Todd tomorrow afternoon.

"Cassie, thanks for calling. But I have to rehearse. Gosh, what if I forget my lines? What should I wear? I just have to be perfect. What if my hair decides at the last minute to have a bad hair day? What if I trip walking up on the stage? What if I didn't emote? What if Todd kisses me and I faint?"

The "what ifs" were endless. Even trying to rehearse was futile after that, because I couldn't focus at all. I could hardly sleep that night. But the next day held even more stress. It was like anticipation and dread at the very same time. Finally 3:15 rolled around, and it was time for me to try out for the role of Juliet. There I was and there was my Romeo, Todd Knowles.

I can only say all my fears were foolish. My hair was great, I didn't trip on stage and I said my lines like a true serious actress. We actually kissed. And yes, I did get the role of Juliet—on stage, and off!

Brianna Reed, 17

"Talking Out-Loud"

The night before her audition, Brianna needed to think clearly about all that she should've done in making sure the next day came off the best it could. What did preparation for the big day with Romeo include? You can bet that Brianna had to do some talking to herself—some "thinking out loud."

"Thinking out loud" is the same skill or technique you use when winding your way through a maze. Think about the process you use to talk to yourself as a way of guiding yourself to the end. If you made a wrong turn you simply stopped, looked ahead, and then tried a new direction. That's the point. A methodical step-by-step way of thinking through what you are going to do, and then self-correcting when you've made a wrong turn, is very helpful when you are in a stressful situation. Here's how Brianna applied the thinking-out-loud skill to her predicament.

"Okay, tomorrow is the big day. I'd better get organized, starting now. I don't want to leave everything until the last minute in the morning. No need to be any more stressed than I already am.

"First, I'll check on my black skirt to see if it's clean.

Here it is. Great, it's clean. I'll wear the striped sweater with it. It's a great look. Looking my best always boosts my confidence.

"I don't want to be rushing around in the morning, so I'll hang my clothes on the back of the door with my black shoes and everything else I'll be wearing, and they'll be ready for me to put on right after I shower in the morning. I'll spend a little extra time on my face tonight, I'd like it to glow tomorrow. I think I'll put on a facial mask while I'm preparing. That   always makes me feel extra pampered.

"I want things to go smoothly tomorrow morning, so I'll go check on what there is to eat for breakfast. I'll need to be thinking and feeling my best so I want to make sure I eat a healthy breakfast. Since I'm slow getting started in the morning, I'll get to bed a half-hour earlier than usual, so that I can wake up a half-hour earlier in the morning and still feel well rested.

"I will definitely reset my alarm clock to give myself plenty of time to spend on getting ready so I won't feel so hurried. I'll study my lines in front of the bathroom mirror one more time before I go to bed and once again in the morning. Being sure that I've done all I can to feel and look my best should help me sleep easier tonight . . . so when Romeo looks for his Juliet tomorrow, I'll be as ready as I can!"

VIRTUAL PRACTICE: TALKING YOUR WAY THROUGH A STRESSFUL SITUATION

You can use the Thinking Out Loud skill to steer yourself through a stressful situation. Think about a real-life dilemma you're facing, and work through it. What will you tell yourself to get yourself through it without adding more stress to an already tense situation?

Coaching yourself along can really help you keep calm and to stay on track toward what ought to be your next move.

Cool is Up To You!

Once you use the self-talk skill, you will use it again and again, because it's quick and easy to apply in those situations where you find yourself harried or scattered. At such times, self-talk provides direction and guidance, allowing you to focus in on the crisis at hand. Of course, sometimes stress is too much to handle on your own, and the best thing is to reach out to those who can give you a hand. The next chapter will help you see why that can be a really good way to approach things.

CHAPTER 11

Reaching Out to Others: Who Are the Members of Your Stress-Management Team?

Having people in our lives who care about us, root for us, and help us feel significant, loved and loving plays a big part in feeling that we can make it through stressful times. Our interdependence with others, and the support we feel from them, helps us feel okay about ourselves—and less diminished—when our lives are burdened by stress and we feel overwhelmed.

This is true even at those times when there is little to nothing you can do about that which is creating stress for you. Things like taking a very big and important test or having a heavy heart because you've just been turned down or rejected by a special someone, or a group of your friends have planned a get together—and didn't invite you—are stress-filled times in which all the love and support from others is not going to make the stress go away.

So how can others take the sting out of the stress you're feeling? It is precisely because there are times when a stressful situation is yours and yours alone that your support system can prove to be most necessary in helping you summon up the personal courage to get through it. That others care about us, and are there to listen and to comfort us, can help us feel that our stress-filled situation is not the end of the world. Feeling "anchored" and "grounded" is to feel bolstered by knowing in overwhelming times, there will be others you can turn to, and who will see your reaching out as a sign of strength.

From family to friends, teachers and coaches, to pets and the face in the mirror, the numbers of those who care about you is, quite possibly, bigger than you may imagine it to be.

Family: Members of the "A" Team

"I love you because I know you so well. I love you despite knowing you so well." Have you ever heard or seen this phrase? It's cute—but meaningful, too. Someone who loves you "warts and all" can be a real asset in times of stress! And who knows you better—inside and out—and still loves you through it all— than family members? The members of families are almost always our number-one fans, as well as our first line of defense in weathering stress. While there certainly can be exceptions, no matter how bad things may seem, those who love us are going to be with us through thick and thin, on our side and in our camp—even when things get tough, and even though we ourselves may not necessarily be at our best.

Perhaps the most important way family members help us cope with the stress and strains of life is this: The love we give and get from our families is important to our feeling wanted, needed and loved—attributes that in the face of life's stresses and strains shield us from feeling alone, without support, even helpless. And while some families may have poor skills in showing love and support—while others have wonderfully positive skills, such as the Buell family in sixteen-year-old Craig Buell's next story—for the most part, our families have the ability to see us through tough times. It's an important consideration.

Psychologists say that teens who have a strong bond with their families, those who feel "anchored" to family, are better able to cope with stress than those who do not. Of course, this does not mean that families are perfect or that family life is without conflict and some stress and strains of its own. Certainly the stress Craig felt was intense and lasted several years. But his situation illustrates how families each have their own unique qualities and their own set of stressful challenges, and shows that just as families can fall apart under stress, they can also pull together to support each other through tough times and incredible challenges.

It's heartening to learn that the most potent way to combat stress is by developing loving bonds with your family—which is a pretty cool thing to know considering that your family are on your team—for life!

Anything but Normal

I'd always thought that I wanted to be (or even just feel) a little different from others my age, just something to stand apart— at least a little. Maybe I felt this way because I was so like everyone in my school and in my neighborhood. I was an ordinary, normal, regular sort of guy. I thought it was a boring existence. Even my family was the typical, but then something happened, and suddenly my family was anything but "normal," Though it started with a doctor's prognosis when I was little, it didn't dawn on me that I got my wish to be "a little different" from all my classmates—or anyone my age, for that matter—all in a moment's realization.

I was only five when my mother returned from an eye exam with news that she didn't need glasses—she needed surgery to remove a tumor that was attached to her pituitary gland. The tumor was the size of a golf ball and could not be totally removed. After her surgery, the doctor advised her to stay in bed for six weeks. During this time, my grandmother came to stay and help my father keep our family's daily life running smoothly. But even with her there, we really missed our mother: We all sort of coped, trying to do for ourselves what our mother had done for us. And we all did our part helping our mother, doing things for her, like taking her meals to her bed and being extra quiet while she was resting so she would get well really soon.

After the sixth week, my grandma left, and each family member took on a little more responsibility to keep things going on as normally as possible. Little by little, Mom did get better, or at least it seemed like she was getting better.

Then, when I was about ten, doctors discovered that the tumor had grown even larger. My mother started radiation treatments to try and stop the tumor from growing, so she wouldn't lose even more of her eyesight. Once again, my grandmother appeared, taking on the role of family caretaker. Once again, we each pitched in to do our part, and hoped our mother would get well—the sooner the better!

But this time, my mother didn't seem to get well—and she just wasn't her usual healthy and happy self. The radiation destroyed her pituitary gland along with, hopefully, the tumor. Now she napped every afternoon and had no energy at night. This was the first time that I realized that there wasn't anything "normal" about my family anymore; feeling terrible was beginning to be "normal" for my mother. Headaches and lack of energy were her most common symptoms, and more and more, there were a lot of little things she could no longer do, like cooking, for example. While my dad took over as head chef, he just can't cook like my mother. No one can cook like my mom, and I really missed all the special things she once made for us—homemade lasagna, for example! Our family sort of "limped along" (as my dad would say when people asked us how we were doing).

There were other things that were not "normal" as they had once been—like the new ban on all friends coming over to the house, because my mother needed so much rest. It was hard to accept that my house would never be the one where all the kids could come and hang out—like Zach Myers's house, for example. His parents let everyone come over, their doors are always open, and all the kids play pool in his family room—his mom even sets out snacks. So while I understood the compromises we made because of my mother's failing health, I resented them, too.

There seemed to be no end to them. Even our family's yearly ritual of going away on a trip together, which included everyone getting to vote on where we were going, changed. Now Mom's health was what mattered most. Would she be comfortable? Would it be safe to take her there—was there a hospital or a medical facility nearby (in case she needed emergency care)? Now it was my father—and not my mother—who was "scout leader," a scout master who had to care for my mother as well as us kids. Our family motto: "Ready, set, charge" was replaced by, "Honey, have you taken all your pills?" Yes, there certainly was a change in our family from once "normal" to now "different" than the other families I knew.

Perhaps *memories* of our trips together underwent the most radical change. Where we once took more pictures than we could possibly use to fill the family album, now we took select pictures, and tried not to photograph our mother when she wasn't feeling her best. Of course, her not being in the photo made her absence really noticeable. Some of the photos were so sad to look at that we didn't even show our mother some of them for fear they would make her self-conscience or sad, like some of the ones we took right before this really bad incident last summer. Compounded by the tumor and having forgotten to take her pills that day, my mother suffered heatstroke. Mom was holding her head as she sat on the ground. My dad took all the water bottles we were carrying and dumped them on her head—and then she recovered and sat in the shade. Needless to say, the photos that were taken that day were sad reminders of a time when, once again, someone we loved so much was so sick.

It's been six years since I was ten and my mother began her radiation treatments. Our whole family's life changed so *drastically*. Given my mother's health condition, and given that we all love each other as we do, we keep making the changes that help each of us cope with our lives—like being involved in lots of school activities, having a lot of friends and dating, too—while still taking care of my mother's special needs. There is no doubt that our family will continue to change: Much of our lives and activities are centered around how my mother is feeling, which varies all the time.

But I've changed, too. I have a better understanding of life, and what it does and doesn't mean to be "normal." I have to admit that there were times when I was resentful of everything, especially my life, revolving around my mother's "health needs."

I don't feel that way any longer. She has been an ill woman and a lucky one, too. If my mother continues the treatments she needs, though her health may not improve, she will live, hopefully to a ripe old age. So for our family, her health care needs are routine, just "the way it is" and in a word, "normal."

I guess you could say I'm "maturing." I've certainly grown into being more understanding and compassionate of my mother's circumstance. Over the last couple years, I've become more aware of the challenges my mother faces with the lack of a pituitary gland, her dependency on drugs and fighting with depression. I know how hard this must be for her. She's the kind of mother who wants the very best for her family, wants to do it all for them, yet her health has made that impossible. I'm sure she tries to keep from us just how hard this has been for her.

I've also developed a greater compassion and respect— even honor—for my father. I can see the toll this has taken on him: the stress of trying to manage the household, be both mother and father, and maintain his job is a heavy load to bear. The medical bills have been huge. I know how much my parents love each other and their children, and I know he must work overtime picking up the slack to make sure we kids get the love and care we need. He's worked hard, and he hasn't complained. He's been a great husband and a wonderful dad.

Finally, being a part of all this has helped me deal with the roller-coaster of first wanting to be anything but normal to then resenting that I didn't have a "normal family." But now, I question if "normal" really exists. The more I talk about my family with my friends, the more I learn how many other kids have special circumstances in their families, too. And when I look around at all the other teenagers everywhere, I wonder what kind of hardships or challenges their family has to face. And I wonder how they feel about it. I wonder if they feel left out of life, or accept their situation as "real life."

So if you're someone who has a challenge like mine that you're keeping a secret—maybe because you feel bad that your family is not normal—know that it's probably more normal than you think. If you talk about it with friends, you'll find that you're not alone, and other teens face challenges in their "normal," families, too. Who knows, maybe some day we will erase the idea of families as "perfect" and look at them in a whole new light—like a place where each member helps each other deal with life, real life. And then, like me, you'll realize that it is the nature of our families and the way each person in it loves and cares for each other (and makes concessions for each other, too) that sets each family apart from others. This is what makes each member special.

So, the next time you look at someone walking up to the front of the room or down the hallway at school, know that even if that person looks like your average sort of person, he or she probably isn't. Know that person has a place in a family and his or her relationship to his or her parents and brothers and sisters and the amount of love that person gets can make a big difference in just who he or she is—whether that person's family is supposedly "normal" or not.

Craig Buell, 16

Four Important Ways Family Members Lessen Your Stress and Make a Big Difference in Your Life

While your family may not have the trials that the Buell family has, most all families do have their own set of challenges. Likewise, each family develops its own "language," its own way to show love, affection and connection.

Because we see them every day, and know that we're going to see them again and again each day, because we count on their being there, it's easy to take our relationships with our family members for granted. But we shouldn't. Instead, we should shower as much love and support on each of our family members as we can.

Here are some of the many ways having a good relationship with family lessens stress.

- **With your family on "your side," the forces of stress seem less significant.** Being a success or failure at school or on the baseball field or with a friend is not the criteria for being welcomed home at the end of the day, for having family members admire you, or for getting (and giving) the love you each need on a daily basis. Even at those times when you've messed up, when you need to "fess up" to something you did that was inappropriate or wrong, you have others in your life who will listen, offer advice and counsel, and support you as you face up to it and come clean. You may be having a really terrible day, but you don't have to depend on that for your sole sense of satisfaction and gratification. You may have failed an important exam, but it's not the end of the world. Having others who love you and care about you and "vote" to have you on the "team" anyway is a great feeling. This love, support, advice and comfort during stressful times helps neutralize stress, making it seem less overwhelming.

- **Parents are your *"fans, not foes,"* a lifeline you can always count on.** Your parents may be easy to get along with, or you may think they are difficult to get along with. You may think of them as fairly lenient in comparison to other parents, or you may think they are overly strict. You may feel it's easy for you to talk with them, or that it's tough to talk with them. For example, it can be scary to tell your parents that you feel in over your head on something—like experimenting with drugs or drinking or even getting bad grades—for fear that they will be upset with you. The truth is, they probably will be upset in the beginning because they may be as overwhelmed and frightened as you. But even if you think they will be upset, even if you feel you have let your parents down, you must tell them anyway. Once they work through their own fears and feelings, they will most always get to work to help you sort things out. Your well-being is their number-one concern, so brave their reaction and know that in the end, your parents usually are the ones who know what's best for you and will do all they can to help you. Just knowing you are not alone and you have your problem out in the open reduces stress, and once your parents are on board, they will help you see it through to the end. Thousands of teens tell us it is their parents they admire most, it is their parents they turn to first in times of real stress and duress—and their parents don't let them down. What an incredible thing to know. In life, you have a lifeline that you can count on.

- **Family members root for you—even when your team loses.** Your brothers and sisters may tease and scream at you, but just let outsiders try to do that! Even though at times you may think your siblings were put on the planet to stress you out, in reality they can be strong members of your stress-coping team. For example, you may constantly argue with your brother or sister over who gets to use the bathroom first. (Sometimes you may even wish you were the only child in the family so you could have it all to yourself!) Still, you know that your brothers and sisters would come to your rescue without a moment's hesitation when you really need it. Once again, you know you have a team: You aren't alone in thinking you are simply the best! Others think so, too.

- **Family offers a place where you get to be just you.** Poet Robert Frost once said, *"Home is where you go and they have to take you in."* While there's always the exception to the rule, for the most part, family always "take you in." They "forgive and forget" more transgressions than most others are willing to do. With family, you get to be who you are—and you'll still belong. There's no struggle to fit in, you are simply a part of the family.

You walk into your home after school and you know you don't have to impress anyone. It can really ease the stress of daily life to know there's a place where you will always be accepted as you are. Sometimes this same freedom to be you is also found in the unconditional love and acceptance of extended family members—with grandparents, aunts, uncles and cousins, for example. As part of their family, you are part of them, and so you're accepted as you are. What a comfort this can be when you may often feel pressured by so many expectations to perform in a certain way, to know there are those with whom acceptance is not based on performance. You, just you; with family, it's enough.

VIRTUAL PRACTICE:
NAMING YOUR "HOME TEAM"

When our relationship with family is strong, it can be a potent source of good feelings and emotional security (a powerful coping tool in the face of stress), as Bob Mortola's example of family support shows.

Bob Mortola, 16, Los Angeles, California

Who: _My Stepdad._

An example of what he did to show me he's on my team:

Yesterday, when I forgot my history paper at home, my stepdad brought it to me at school, even though he had to take time to his leave his office, go home and then drive to my school.

How that buffered stress for me: _He wasn't angry, and he didn't lecture me about being forgetful. He was concerned that I be able to turn in an assignment I'd worked so hard on in time to get a good grade on it._

How having a good relationship with my stepdad makes me more resilient to stress: *It makes me feel like I'm not alone with whatever stress I have to face, and it gives me a safe place to go to when I'm feeling overwhelmed.*

How about for you? Think about each member of your family, and consider how that person is on "your team." How does having a good relationship with that person buffers stress for you?

Cool is Up To You!

It's much easier to get through times of stress with your family on your side. Do your part to keep these relationships strong and loving. Not only can they run interference against the blows of stress now, they'll also cheer you on for a long time to come.

CHAPTER 12

Friends: On the Team—and the Pep Squad, Too!

While learning to be a part of "the team" begins in the family, it most definitely gets refined in "hanging out" with our friends. Good friends listen to us, hear us out, are there to pal around with and, in general, just enjoy being with us—which is what makes them friends in the first place! Friends who care about you and look out for you make for VIPs (Very Important Persons) when it comes to being members of your stress-management team.

The term team is particularly significant when we think of friends. We live in a world with others, and just about everything we do is done in concert with people. We live in families and within communities; we go to school and work with others. We communicate with people on a daily basis. Just as we experience the pleasure, fun and joy of being with others, should they be experiencing disappointment, upset or pain in their lives, we can feel it and be stressed by it, too. Certainly this was true for fifteen-year-old Gina Rivera (in the following story), whose best friend faced a life-threatening crisis—one that caused Gina to examine not only the friendship the two girls shared, but the extent to which she would go in order to help a friend choose victory over the challenge she faced, regardless of whether or not the friend approved.

Having a Couple of Friends is Better than Just One

Kayla and Sara are both friends, of mine, but they're very different. For instance, the other day the three of us were going to go to the movies. "Do I look okay?" I asked Sara.

Without even so much as looking at me, she replied, "Yeah, sure. You always look great."

"How about my hair?"

"Yeah. Looks great," she responded.

The moment Kayla walked in, she took one look at me and demanded, "You're not going to be seen in that, are you? No way am I going to be seen with you if you wear that!"

"What's wrong with it?" I asked.

"Well, for one thing, you look like a little kid in it, and for another, there's a mustard stain on the left sleeve." She paused, frowned and then added, "Having a bad hair day?"

You can see how different they are. Sara is a person who doesn't want to upset you, so she always says something nice and would never want to make you feel uneasy, no matter what. Kayla is very blunt and outspoken. She has very definite opinions and isn't afraid to be honest. Kayla is definitely not afraid to say what she thinks. So, if I really really want to know how I look, while I ask them both, it's Kayla's advice that's worth the most. She has no problem telling me her honest opinion about anything. If the way I look passes her inspection, I can be sure that it will pass with others. Now, if I was worried about a big test at school, I'd go to Sara for help. Kayla puts as little energy as possible into her grades. Sara, on the other hand, is very smart, understands what it's like to want to get good grades, and will help you out when you need it. Both Karla and Sara are good friends, each in her own way.

Friends. They're so different. That's why you need lots of them.

Barbara Allen, 14

4 Ways Friends Create—and Help You Make It Through—Stressful Times

You know firsthand that friends, while they're one of the first you turn to in times of stress, are a source of stress as well! Why? Because having friends is one of the most important mirrors we have. Here are four reasons that friends both create some of the stress we feel and can be the antidote to stress as well.

✓ **With friends, we "belong."** To be accepted by others, and to feel as if we belong, supports our natural instincts for self-acceptance, making us feel whole and complete. Having friends means that we are a part of something. This sense of belonging is a powerful contribution to how secure, happy and content we are. The happier we are, the better we weather the strains and pressures of life. And of course, when we feel left out or rejected by friends, well, that's a big source of stress. Losing a friend can be even more devastating. Losing a friend is simply a major loss: A friend offers understanding and acceptance during a time when we struggle to understand and accept ourselves. They like us in spite of our acne, braces, the D- on the quiz—and even that fib we told. How can we possibly navigate life.

✓ **Having friends means we aren't alone.** A big part of the experience of being a teenager is exploring the world, a world spent away from your home and parents, even your own neighborhood. You're out there in school and in life, doing things for the first time and learning to do things your own way. It just wouldn't be fun to do those things all alone, so having someone to do them with is important. A good friend makes these experiences more than just fun; a good friend adds to them in just about every way. Perhaps, most important, in a world that can seem so big and overwhelming, friends offer us the comfort of connection, with friends, we're not in it alone! Walking down the hall in school alone, with all eyes on you, may be okay now and then, but it's an intimidating experience. But when you're walking down that same hall with your friend at your side, well, you just feel like you can take on, or fend off, the whole world.

✓ **Parents love you, but friends help you out; they share *in the experience*.** Friends have the same kinds of situations as you, so they serve as a comparison for you and your life. Friends help each other see if the world looks to others as it does to you—or not. It's confirmation, a baseline by which to gauge how you are doing.

It's the "I know what you're going through," and the "I'm just as scared (or confident) as you are." The feedback of friends seems more real and authentic—because friends are right there with you. Times of stress are shared in this way, and the stress is lessened.

✓ Friends listen to each other and console one another. Sometimes this means keeping each others' secrets, big and small, having someone who sees you at the top of your game and at your very lowest.

VIRTUAL PRACTICE: WHO AMONG YOUR FRIENDS HELPS YOU THROUGH STRESS?

Are your friends members of your stress management team? Identify those who are "on your team." Ask:

- Who is always "there" for me?
- Who listens to me when I just need to talk?
- Who can I talk to, about anything and everything, and know for sure they won't share what I've told them with anyone else?

- Who really cares about me and wants what is best for me?
- Who makes me feel better when I'm feeling down?

We asked Morgan to complete this exercise, too, and we've provided it here as an example.

Friend: _Gina Rivera_

How do I know she/he is on my team? _Gina kept my secret about my anorexia for a long time, but when she got concerned, she did all she could to see I got the help and support I needed to get back on track with my health. Not only did she tell me how worried she was about me, she talked to her mother and the school nurse, which I know couldn't have been easy for her._

How my friend helps me cope with stress: _Gina listens, she gives me good advice, she will always tell me the truth. Because of her, I got the help I needed._

Who among your friends would you name to your stress-management team and how he or she helps you weather the stress and pressures in your life?

Cool is Up To You!

Having friends who are there for you to help you work things through—even by just being a listening ear—is a real source of support when dealing with a tough issue or stressful time. Friends are a real asset; be sure to be considerate of their feelings. If you want to have friends, be one. Like the proverb says, "To have a friend, you have to be a friend."

CHAPTER 13
Prevention and Intervention Skills:
Great Ways to Take Care of Yourself

Dear Adam,

We know that you are going through a lot of stress right now and hurting too much to know the right thing to do. But drinking and using drugs is really not helping, and is only making things worse. We're sorry that our trying to "talk some sense into you" the other day turned into a yelling match; we were only trying to get you to see how self-destructive drinking and drugs are to your coping with your life. We want you to know we are not down on you, and that we just want you to be okay. So many people care about you, even though it may seem like they've given up hope that you'll be the same person we once knew and liked so much. We want you to know we're here for you, and we hope you'll take better care of yourself. We want our Adam back.

Your good friends,

Tommy L.,
Candi M., Tara S.

Adam Harris is really fortunate to have friends like Tommy, Candi and Tara. Surely their friendship and support mean a lot to him, especially at a time when he is potentially facing addiction. But in addition to the friendship and support of his friends—and their plea that he get some help—Adam will have to choose this, too. Just as you want others to be supportive of you, especially when going through stressful times, you've got to want to take care of yourself, as well. Up to now, your parents and teachers and other adults have looked out for you and your wellbeing. But you're a teenager now and growing wise enough to assume much of the responsibility for your well-being— especially as it relates to eating nutritiously, getting the rest and exercise you need, and doing those things that help you become a caring and competent person.

A large part of assuming responsibility means taking charge. It means that you can count on yourself to make the right and best choices for all the things that are a part of your life. For example, maybe you've been in the habit of doing things only when pressed to do them, such as starting on your homework or assigned family chores only when reminded (for the second time)! Taking care of yourself means that you no longer have to be told to get your homework done. After all, you know that if you don't, the next day you are not going to be prepared for your work (school) day.

Taking care of yourself is a "bigger and better" idea than saying, "Gosh, if I don't get my homework done, my parents and teachers will be upset with me." Now that you're a teenager, you can take charge of your life in many ways. One of them is to take good care of yourself— and not always make it someone else's responsibility for overseeing that you do. Taking care of yourself.

What does that mean? Here are twelve things teens listed as among the most important.

1. **Take good care of your body.** Don't take risks that could put your safety and your health in jeopardy (such as using drugs and alcohol).

2. **Take good care of your mental health.** Don't let the opinions and comments of others be more important than how you feel about yourself. Take care of your self-esteem; believe that the image (reputation) you hold of yourself is more important than what others think of you. No one else knows you as you know you, so believe in yourself. Treat yourself with respect, and as though you are your own best friend.

3. **Think about your life, and what you want out of it.** Don't think that your life just happens to you, and that you have no control over anything in it. Think about what you want, and make a plan and go for it. Why waste your life; why act like you are powerless to do anything for yourself?

4. **Don't be thrown off by life's daily ups and downs.** Accept that a certain amount of confusion and turmoil are common to everyone at all ages—even for those teens around whose lives

appear to be "all roses." We all, at one time or another, feel unsure of ourselves, confused and even a little lost. These times pass. When times are tough, take extra good care of yourself. And don't forget to reach out for help if you need it.

5. **Make choices consistent with values you know to be good and right, those you can be proud to stand up for.**

6. **Find out who you are and what makes you tick.** Learn about yourself—your personality, your talents and what makes you happy.

7. **Set worthy goals and strive to achieve them.**

8. **Practice your faith.** Faith is about the timeless truths and provides leadership to your heart and soul—the core of your being.

9. **Learn all you can, about all that you can.** Read broadly and expose yourself to great minds. This allows you to examine your own assumptions, and to check your biases. Keep an open mind.

10. **Be respectful, considerate and friendly to others.** Accept differences. We are each making our way through life the best way we know how. We are all learning as we go. No one has the "only way." We are doing the best we can with what we have.

11. **When you screw up, admit it, apologize and then forgive yourself.** You will find others are willing to cut you some slack, especially if you are good-natured and courteous—so be sure to do this for yourself. It's only natural that sometimes you'll mess up. When this happens, admit it, talk about it, apologize for your shortcomings, and then vow to do better. Then let go and move on.

12. **Talk to others about how things are going for you.** Sharing things with others can not only lighten the load of the stress you're feeling, but help you see that everyone has tough times. When you talk about how you—and they—got through things, you'll feel better about yourself and be more confident in getting through the next "crisis"—and there will be others.

We think these twelve suggestions are insightful, and good advice. Certainly they are very important in your goal to minimize—even prevent—the normal stress and pressures of life. Here are some other ways to take care of yourself so that you are at your best.

The Importance of Nutrition and Sleep

As powerful and durable as the body is, it also a very sensitive and delicate machine. If you fuel it with all the nutrients it needs to keep running, it will hum right along with the schedule you keep. But if you fail to give it the nutrition it needs, it won't perform at peak efficiency. For example, if you give it an extra dose of pasta, its gears shift into slow, very slow; give it an extra dose of sugar, and its gears shift into high—as in, running out of control.

If you provide your body with the rest it needs, it will restore itself day after day, for years on end. If you fail to give it the sleep it needs, it will be sluggish, and may even go to sleep while on the job. It you give it more sleep than it needs, it may also be sluggish and unwilling to "get going." If you keep all its delicate and intricate parts in working order, via exercise, it will stay in top form and amaze you with its strength and energy. If you fail to give it the exercise it needs, it will be lazy and weak.

The body is an amazing machine, one that is also sensitive to stress, most teens discover.

Going to school, dealing with friends and teachers, homework and part-time jobs—all are just a few ways that teen life makes for stressful times. But while you can't prevent stress, there are things you can do to be at your best so that you are as prepared as you can be. Eating nutritious foods, getting adequate exercise and rest head the list.

Food Is the Body's Fuel:
Three Ways "High Octane" Combats Stress

Eating nutritiously is your body's best and first line of defense in combating stress. What you eat affects your moods, energy level, how you feel, think and make decisions—all important to dealing with pressure-filled situations.

Nutrition can sometimes seem like a not-so-important, even a "ho-hum" issue. I mean, if you select the burger instead of the salad at lunch, you aren't going to collapse on the floor, right? And it can be difficult to connect eating healthy foods with whether or not that special someone is going to ask you to the dance, right? Still, there is a definite relationship between what you eat and how you handle the stress of when that special someone asks you out, or when he or she doesn't—to say nothing of how you handle all those stress-filled moments waiting to see which it will be.

The expression, "you are what you eat," has a lot of merit when it comes to coping with the demands of stress. Here are three ways nutrition is related to how you cope with stress.

1. The way you fuel your body—the foods you eat—has a definite effect on how you feel (calm, energized, tired, irritable, sluggish, even hyper) and thus how you are able to cope with your day. As an example, have you ever only eaten a couple of sugar-coated donuts for breakfast? You probably felt an initial burst of hyper-energy from all the sugar, but by lunchtime your energy was no doubt dragging. A stressful situation demands your attention and if you aren't up for it, you won't bring your best efforts to confrontation and resolution. Whether in the middle of a hyper-energy sugar rush or an energy-zapped droop, you won't be at your best in coping with the stress at hand. Let's say you're coping with the usual agenda of a million-and-one things to do, plus the excitement of being with friends, keeping up with the demands of school and the like, and then let's toss in an unexpected stressor—like an upset with a best friend, a flat tire or a pop quiz. If you're feeling good and up for the day, chances are, while being inconvenienced and throwing your day off schedule, you're not likely to go into a stressed-out frenzy or crash into tears. What's more, you'll be able to think clearly so you can better figure out solutions to the problem at hand. If you haven't adequately fueled your body—let's say you're on a sugar high or drooping, then you're not going to do too well with this added strain. You may even end up creating more problems with your stress-induced reactions.

2. When you're under stress, you need your body to cope with the physical demands you make on it. When the body is deprived of essential nutrients, it doesn't function as it should (such as having a good energy supply). This means you'll be less capable of withstanding the effects of stress—not to mention less capable of keeping up with your schedule. Health and nutrition experts say teen girls need about 2,500 to 2,700 calories a day, and that teen boys need about 2,800 to 3,000 calories daily—just to meet the demands of a growing body. But there is quite a distinction between a "good calorie" and an "empty calorie." If your 3,000 calories come from candy bars, this will not meet your body's need to run efficiently. Nor will it help you withstand the effects of stress.

    In all, your body needs about forty-seven different nutritional substances to sustain itself. Vegetables, whole grain or enriched cereals and breads, a form of protein (such as beans and lean meat) and milk all help the body function properly. Medical experts and nutritionists agree that eating a balanced diet is the best way to get the proper mix of nutrients.

(A diet that emphasizes one type of food—whether proteins, vegetables or carbohydrates— to the exclusion of other foods is harmful to the body because it deprives the body of the balance it needs to function efficiently.)

3. **Brain cells, like the rest of the body, require proper feeding in order to function correctly.** The brain is the body's most chemically sensitive organ. When deprived of proper nutrients, the brain cannot perform at peak efficiency. Too much sugar or vitamin deficiencies can seriously disrupt the brain's ability to function normally and effectively.

   Remember the goal: Use food to help your body be at its best. When you're facing a stressful time, such as a really big exam or semester finals, or you're trying out for the tennis team, or today is the day you really must break up (or make up) with someone, start your day with a high-energy breakfast and then feed it nutritious foods throughout the day. If your "stress attack" exam starts at 2:00 and you're not only tired but famished, eat a high-energy bar or a piece of fruit. If your energy is flagging, rather than grabbing a bag of cookies or chips from the dispenser, buy an energy bar or bag of nuts instead.

   The important thing is to eat foods that will feed your growing body, as well as provide energy to sustain your activities and help you manage the stress and pressures of life.

5 Stress-Busting Benefits of Exercise

The powerful machine that it is, the body needs exercise to stay strong and run efficiently. One obvious benefit of exercise is having buffed muscles, but exercise is also extremely important in helping you buffer the effects of stress. Here are five ways exercise can help you become more resilient to stress:

- **Exercise relaxes nerves and balances emotions.** Have you ever gone for a jog or a bike ride when you're feeling really stressed-out and tense? If you have, chances are you noticed that you felt much more relaxed afterwards. That's because exercise burns off pent-up stress, and therefore, relaxes nerves, which in turn, balances emotions.

- **Exercise increases your intake of oxygen, which improves your (physical and mental) alertness.** This in turn, helps you think more clearly—and, of course, the more clearly you can think, the better you are able to deal with stress. One way to get the type of workout that will increase your oxygen in this way also happens to be a great way to burn off the tension of stress—aerobic exercise. "Aerobic" means a level of activity that requires you to exert a good deal of effort, but doesn't consume oxygen faster than your heart and lungs can supply it. In keeping our bodies working efficiently and effectively on the inside, experts recommend three sessions of vigorous activity weekly, with each session lasting from twenty to thirty minutes. (You will be pleased to know that even a twenty-or thirty-minute impromptu game of basketball— or dancing— can provide the exercise you need to burn off stress and increase your oxygen levels.)

- **Exercise heightens your energy level.** When you're feeling fatigued, it's more difficult to cope with stress. Exercise can help chase away fatigue because, while exercising burns energy, it also restores it. Have you ever been in a slump at school— just so tired you'd like to go home and forget your last-period class—when a friend comes along and starts a game of tag with you, and presto! After even a few minutes, you find your fatigue has evaporated and you're magically invigorated.

- **Exercise improves your sense of well-being.** When you exercise, not only are you getting endorphins (our bodies' own mood lifters), but you're also doing something good for yourself: Between the increase in your body's endorphins and the added oxygen to your brain, you'll notice a sense of well-being. When you feel good about yourself and your life, those things that might otherwise stress you out seem less threatening, less looming, less "do or die."

- Exercise improves your quality of sleep. You've gone hiking with friends and had a great workout; that night you crawl under your covers and get the best night of sleep you can imagine. Exercise actually helps you get a good night's sleep. When your body has had the rest it needs, you are more likely to find effective ways to cope with it—rather than to feel so overwhelmed by it that it simply debilitates you. Getting the sleep that you need helps set you up for your best coping possibilities; in short, you'll do better managing it effectively.

The good news is that there are all kinds of ways to get a good workout, and that can be interesting, even fun. From playing sports at school to working out at the fitness center; from running to in-line skating (or Rollerblading); from kick-boxing to dancing—all qualify as exercise and build your resilience to stress. It's nice to know you're not limited to jumping jacks; you can dance to your favorite CD while watching TV! Now that's not a hardship! Then, after spending all that energy, you'll have an even greater reason to chill and relax (which is also an important tool in keeping your cool when stressed).

SLEEP: Stress and Your Zzzzz's

Does the subject of getting all the sleep you need sound like information that would put you to sleep? It shouldn't. Sleep is so vital to your well-being that you can't function without it. Besides waking up fresh the next day and being able to handle things, like coping with the stress and pressures on a daily basis, here are three reasons that getting enough sleep is so important:

- **A rested body is key to being alert and on top of things.** Have you ever found yourself to be too tired to be patient and sort things out? If so, did you make things worse by ignoring the problem, or overreact, all because you were tired and not at your best? Health experts say that teens need between eight and twelve hours of sleep to maintain the intense stage of growth and development. Consider in addition to the demands of a growing body the toll of stress in coping with teen life!

- **Sleep is your body's recovery period.** During sleep your muscles relax, your breathing and heart rates decrease, and your body temperature drops slightly. This recovery period primes your body to withstand stress. But not all sleep is the same.

  There are actually two different types of sleep: non-rapid eye movement (NREM) and rapid eye movement (REM). This sounds complicated, but it really isn't. In NREM, the "best sleep," your eyes move very little and your body reaches its state of deepest relaxation. NREM has four stages, each stage taking the body into a deeper and deeper phase of sleep, the last of these phases offering the body its best rest (primarily because the muscles in your entire body are most relaxed). Because it is during a state of deep relaxation that the body renews itself, the NREM stage of sleep is very important to the health of the body. Fitness experts tell us that people who exercise regularly and are in a relaxed state upon going to bed spend more time in the NREM state of sleep than those who don't exercise. In REM, which makes up about 25 percent of your sleeping time, the brain is still at a high level of brain activity. This is the stage of sleep in which you dream.

- **Sleep is how the body renews itself.** Your body needs sleep. You've probably noticed a certain pattern to your body's ability to meet the demands of your life on a daily basis. For example, you probably wake up about the same time, get hungry around the same times each day, and get tired pretty much about the same time each evening. We call this twenty-four-hour cycle of energy flow the circadian rhythm. Even your temperature, mood and alertness tend to rise and fall at roughly the same time every day. In other words, your body likes a predictable "routine"—such as going to bed at the same time each night, or even looking at your watch when it's lunch time. When your body experiences the comfort and renewal of this routine, it is less susceptible to both the physical and emotional effects of stress.

Are you getting all the sleep you need? Here are some things you can do to help ensure a restful night's sleep.

- Make sure you are getting adequate exercise. There is nothing like the rest that comes from the body being tired and wanting to rest itself.
- Go to bed at the same time every night. The body likes a routine, one it can count on.
- Don't play heavy metal or music with a fast tempo just prior to going to bed. This music will "rev" you up. Save it for the morning or after school when your goal is to re-energize. Instead, when getting ready for bed, put on soothing and relaxing sounds. This helps clear your mind of your schedule and hectic day.
- Fill your mind with uplifting, pleasant and reassuring thoughts, those that can help you wind down your day, and prepare to get the rest you need to have a great tomorrow. The goal is to relax so you can get to sleep.
- Don't eat right before bedtime. You don't want your body to have to work at digesting food when you are trying to shut down for the night.
- Avoid stimulants such as caffeine, sugar and nicotine. These will keep you awake.
- Create a soothing surrounding. Choose soothing colors for your walls, decorate with your favorite pictures and snapshots of family and friends, and your favorite stuffed animals.

VIRTUAL PRACTICE:
FOOD, BOD AND ZZZZZ'S

1. "You are what you eat." How have you witnessed this expression in your daily life? _____

    _____

    _____

2. Describe a time when you were stressed, and exercise reduced the stress you were feeling. _____

    _____

    _____

3. What is the one most important thing you can do to improve the quality of sleep you get on a daily basis? _____

    _____

    _____

Cool is Up To You!

Nutrition, exercise and sleep are key to our ability to deal with stress. In the next chapter, you'll learn how breathing right can also help you rid yourself of stress, and prevent it as well.

CHAPTER 14

Prevention and Intervention Skills:
Cool Ways to Chill Out
(and Relax)

Have you ever been so stressed-out that you couldn't eat, sleep, relax—even think straight? Learning to relax can help you break the spell of stress.

3 Cool Reasons to Melt Stress via Relaxation

When the pressure you feel is overwhelming, it can be helpful to take a step back from the situation, and just let go of the stress—to really relax. Not only does this kind of relaxation help you renew your energy, it helps you ease up on the building aches of knotting muscles. Here are some other important reasons to learn the art of relaxation.

1. **Relaxation is an antidote to "overwhelm."** When you relax you are able to sort out your thoughts and feelings and come to a clearer, more manageable view of what's going on in your world and emotions. It helps you get a better perspective. Being able to sort things out this way helps you feel less overwhelmed and better able to deal with the task or stress at hand.

2. **Relaxation can "unstress" tense muscles.** Often when you are nervous, upset or afraid, your muscles get tense or tight. Sometimes they stay that way for a while—like a few hours or days, long after the stressful event. This tension can lead to headaches, muscle aches and cramps. Relaxing soothes muscles, helping you feel less tense, less irritable and you therefore feel better able to manage yourself.

3. **Relaxation keeps you from looking like a Grinch.** When you're under stress, do you look as though you have steam coming from your ears? Are the words "stressed out!" stamped on your forehead? Do your eyes pull down, looking sad? Stress can be seen in the face, the muscles and the posture. Try this. Think about a time when you were really upset. Now stand in front of the mirror and think about that incident. Are your legs in a defensive stance? Is your jaw tight? Not a very attractive sight, is it? Learning to relax keeps you from looking like a close relative of the Grinch.

Mental Imagery: Reducing "Brain Strain"

Do you ever find yourself in a daydream, even while a flurry of activities are going on around you? You probably thought not being able to concentrate on the task at hand—especially when something important is going on around you, like the teacher giving a lecture on algorithms, or your parents laying out the new rules for curfew— meant you had a poor attention span. Au contraire! Hold on to that skill! Yes, skill.

If you are successful at taking short trips in your mind, you already know a great way to reduce the (brain) strain of stress.

Mental Imagery: Reducing "Brain Strain"

Here are four ways that using mental imagery reduces your stress:

- **Mental imagery directs your thoughts to a more positive perspective.** When you are able to visualize a beautiful place and outcome, it helps you open to a more positive perspective. Being able to hold a vision of calm helps you move towards solutions and away from the problem and the stress of thinking about it.

- **Mental imagery calms your emotions.** When your thoughts are directed towards a more positive perspective, you feel more calm and hopeful. Your stress is lowered as your confidence in your ability to cope and succeed is raised.

- **Mental imagery helps you relax mind and body in tense situations.** We already know how the mind and the body are connected when it comes to stress: well, when you visualize paradise and good with the mind, the body comes along for the ride. The calm images, outcomes and scenarios your mind creates seep into the body, easing away tension.

- **Mental imagery improves your ability to find creative ways out of a jam.** Have you ever been in a spot (like Mom or Dad give you a lecture, and your mind took a little time out) and thought of a very creative way to get out of the jam? Very useful, right? Maybe the time you were "taking a mental break" you actually did come up with a creative solution. As you visualize, you are better able to come to creative solutions for coping with stress.

VIRTUAL PRACTICE: HOW TO TRAIN YOUR MIND
TO TAKE A MINI-VACATION

To begin using visualization to help you stay "cool" in the heat of stress, simply think of the most beautiful, serene setting you can imagine and place yourself right there in the middle of that setting. Try to experience the scene in every way you can, including the use of images from your senses—such as smell (for example, the scent of flowers), touch (the feel of the grass beneath your feet), sound (the sound of birds singing in the trees), and taste (the salt air at the beach). And by the way, you can also use soothing music along with this exercise to create a calm state. Be patient with yourself as you begin to learn mental relaxation. Don't get too concerned if at first your mind wanders off to other places. Simply redirect your thoughts. Following are some helpful step-by-step tips:

Step 1:   Find a quiet place without distractions.

Step 2:   Sit or lie down and get comfortable and loosen any tight-fitting clothing.

Step 3:   Close your eyes.

Step 4:   Take a deep breath. Imagine breathing in the clean air. As you breathe out, feel the relaxation spread over your body. As you take another breath, feel yourself floating down.

Step 5   Tense and relax your muscles.

Step 6:   Imagine or picture yourself doing something relaxing (such as soothing your pet, picking flowers, floating peacefully in a swimming pool, relaxing by the fireplace).

Step 7:   When you are finished, stretch your arms, take a deep breath and open your eyes.

Mental maps for your imaginary journey to a place that is stress free: What a great (and inexpensive) journey.

Cool is Up To You!

When you find yourself feeling stressed-out over a problem, see yourself dealing with it successfully. When you do this, you have a much better chance of being in charge of your emotions, which makes you much more likely to be in control of your behavior. Being in charge of your emotions and being able to control your behavior is sure to lower your stress.

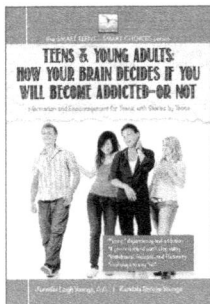

How Your Brain Decides If You Will Become Addicted—Or Not
Information and Encouragement for Teens, with Stories by Teens
Jennifer Leigh Youngs, A.A. / Kendahl Brooke Youngs

- *"using," dependency and addiction*
- *if you or a friend can't stop using*
- *Withdrawal, Relapse, and Recovery*
- *cool ways to say "no"*

Book: 978-1-940784-99-1
e-book: 978-1-940784-98-4

The 10 Commandments and the Secret Each One Guards—For You
Information and Inspiration about Faith at Work in Our lives
Bettie B. Youngs, Ph.D., Ed.D. / Jennifer Leigh Youngs, A.A.

- *how the Commandments speak to you*
- *the secret each Commandment guards*
- *using your faith to guide the choices you make*
- *how to be confident and bold in your faith*

Book: 978-1-940784-95-3
e-book: 978-1-940784-94-6

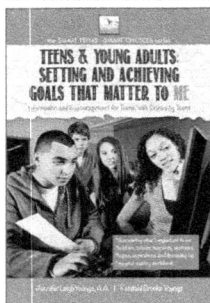

Setting and Achieving Goals that Matter to ME
Information and Encouragement for Teens, with Stories by Teens
Jennifer Leigh Youngs, A.A. / Kendahl Brooke Youngs

- *discovering what's important TO ME*
- *hobbies, talents, interests, apptitudes*
- *hopes, aspirations and dreaming big*
- *my goal-setting workbook*

Book: 978-1-940784-97-7
e-book: 978-1-940784-96-0

How to Be Courageous
Inspirational Short Stories and Encouragement for Teens, by Teens
Jennifer Leigh Youngs, A.A. / Kendahl Brooke Youngs

- *the importance of being caring*
- *the benefits of being brave*
- *how to be a hero*

Book: 978-1-940784-93-9
e-book: 978-1-940784-92-2

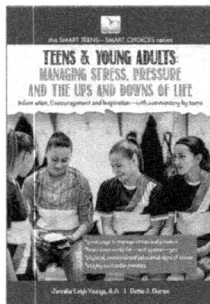

Managing Stress, Pressure, and the Ups and Downs of Life
Information, Encouragement and Inspiration—with commentary by teens
Jennifer Leigh Youngs, A.A. / Bettie J. Burres

- *great ways to manage stress and pressure*
- *how stress works for—and against—you*
- *physical, emotional and behavioral signs of stress*
- *staying cool under pressure*

Book: 978-1-940784-80-9
e-book: 978-1-940784-81-6

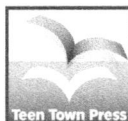

TEEN TOWN PRESS
www.TeenTownPress.com

www.BettieYoungsBooks.com
info@BettieYoungsBooks.com

Foreign Rights Representation: Sylvia Hayse Literary Agency, LLC
sylvia@SylviaHayseLiterary.com | C: 1.541.404.3127

www.ingramcontent.com/pod-product-compliance
Lightning Source LLC
Chambersburg PA
CBHW021345090426
42742CB00008B/757